*pathfinder® guide*

D1150308

# More Cotswold

# WALKS

*Compiled by*
*Brian Conduit*

JARROL
publish

## Acknowledgements

My thanks for the valuable advice and numerous useful leaflets that I obtained from the various tourist information centres throughout the area. Also I am grateful for the help given by the National Trust in planning Walk 23 through Sherborne Park.

| | |
|---|---|
| Text: | Brian Conduit |
| Photography: | Brian Conduit and Jarrold Publishing |
| Editorial: | Ark Creative, Norwich |
| Design: | Ark Creative, Norwich |

Series Consultant:     Brian Conduit

© Jarrold Publishing, an imprint of Pitkin Publishing Ltd

Ordnance Survey® This product includes mapping data licensed from Ordnance Survey the Controller of Her Majesty's Station Copyright 2006. All rights reserved. Li Ordnance Survey, the OS symbol and I trademarks and Explorer, Landranger ; trademarks of the Ordnance Survey, th agency of Great Britain.

Jarrold Publishing

ISBN 978-0-7117-1118-1

While every care has been taken to er of the route directions, the publishers responsibility for errors or omissions, or for changes in details given. The countryside is not static: hedges and fences can be removed, field boundaries can alter, footpaths can be rerouted and changes in ownership can result in the closure or diversion of some concessionary paths. Also, paths that are easy and pleasant for walking in fine conditions may become slippery, muddy and difficult in wet weather, while stepping stones across rivers and streams may become impassable.

If you find an inaccuracy in either the text or maps, please write to or e-mail Jarrold Publishing at the addresses below.

First published 2000 by Jarrold Publishing
Revised and reprinted 2006.

Printed in Belgium. 3/07

**Pitkin Publishing Ltd**
Healey House, Dene Road, Andover, Hampshire SP10 2AA
email: info@totalwalking.co.uk
www.totalwalking.co.uk

**Front cover:** The Churn Valley
**Previous page:** Owlpen Manor, near Dursley, Gloucestershire

# Contents

The National Trust; The Ramblers' Association; Walkers and the Law; Countryside Access Charter; Walking Safety; The Cotswold Voluntary Warden Service; Useful Organisations; Ordnance Survey Maps

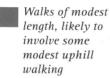

■ Short, easy walks

■ Walks of modest length, likely to involve some modest uphill walking

■ More challenging walks which may be longer and/or over more rugged terrain, often with some stiff climbs

# Keymap 1

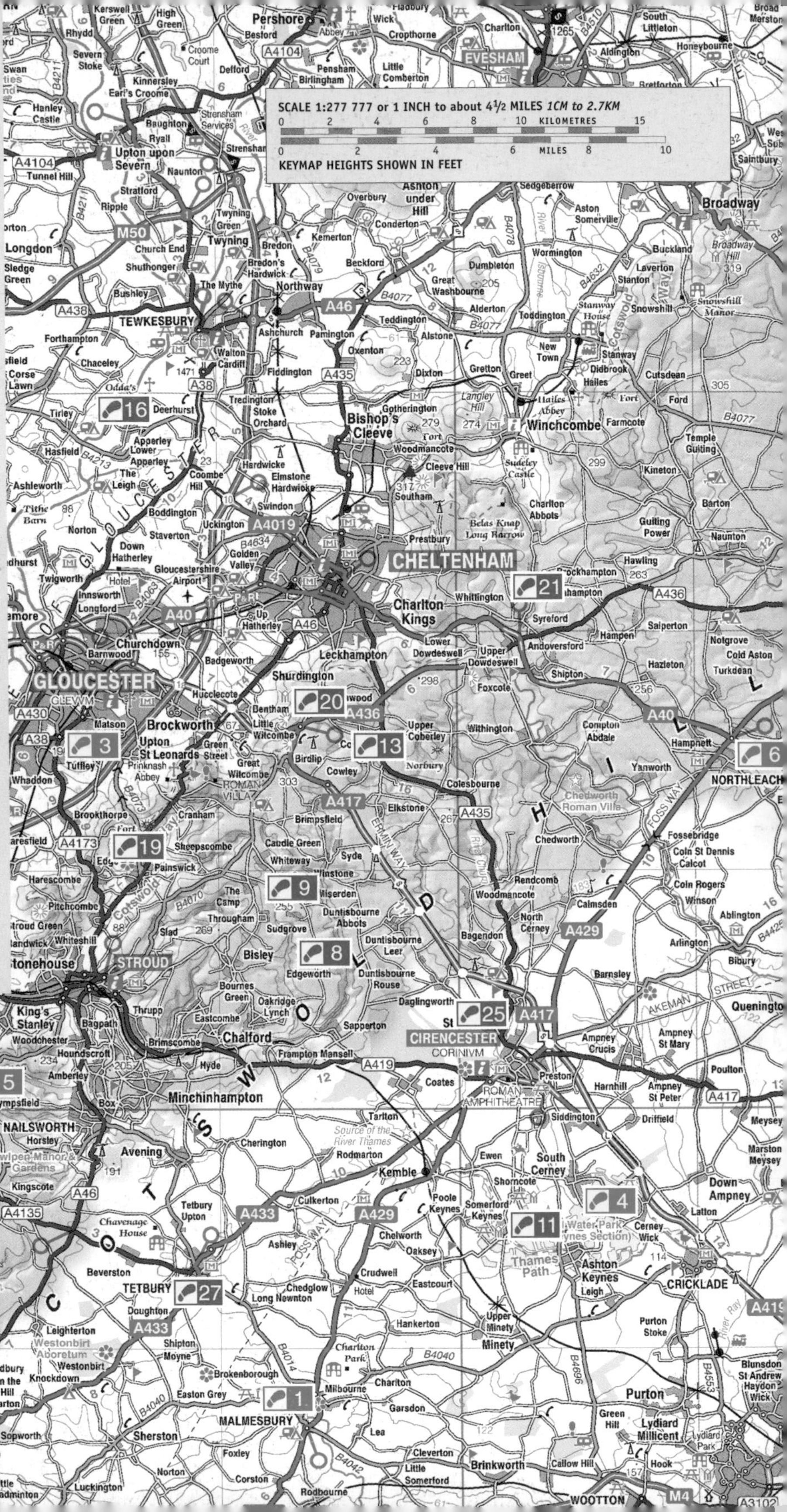

SCALE 1:277 777 or 1 INCH to about 4½ MILES 1CM to 2.7KM

0  2  4  6  8  10  KILOMETRES  15

0  2  4  MILES  8  10

KEYMAP HEIGHTS SHOWN IN FEET

EVESHAM

Broadway

TEWKESBURY

Winchcombe

CHELTENHAM

Charlton Kings

GLOUCESTER

Brockworth

NORTHLEACH

STROUD

CIRENCESTER
CORINIVM

Chalford

Minchinhampton

NAILSWORTH

Avening

Kemble

South Cerney

Ashton Keynes

CRICKLADE

TETBURY

MALMESBURY

Purton

WOOTTON

SWINDON · BANBURY · Chipping Campden · Moreton-in-Marsh · Stow-on-the-Wold · Chipping Norton · Woodstock · Witney · Burford · Carterton · Faringdon · Lechlade on Thames · Fairford · Highworth · Wantage · Grove · Charlbury · Eynsham · Bampton · Shrivenham · Watchfield · Stratton St Margaret · Harwell · Marcham · Bloxham · Deddington · Shipston-on-Stour · Middle Tysoe · Bourton-on-the-Water · Stanford in the Vale

Numbered markers: 2 · 26 · 10 · 14 · 18 · 23 · 12 · 7 · 24 · 17

*Keymap 2*

CHELTENHAM

21

6

23

12

24

25 A417

CIRENCESTER
CORINIVM

4

11

17

NORTHLEACH

BURFORD

CARTERTON

FAIRFORD

LECHLADE ON THAMES

FARINGDON

HIGHWORTH

Shrivenham

Watchfield

CRICKLADE

A419

SWINDON

A4311

Stratton St Margaret

A420

WOOTTON BASSETT

M4

A3102

Wroughton

Chiseldon

Aldbourne

Lyneham

Brinkworth

Ogbourne St George

Ogbourne St Andrew

A346

Avebury

CALNE

Marlborough Downs

Avebury Stone Circles,
West Kennett Stone Avenue

A346

SCALE 1:277 777 or 1 INCH to about 4½ MILES  *1CM to 2.7KM*

0  2  4  6  8  10  KILOMETRES  15

0  2  4  6  MILES  8  10

KEYMAP HEIGHTS SHOWN IN FEET

*At-a-glance...*

| Walk | Page | Start | Nat. Grid Reference | Distance | Time | Highest Point |
|------|------|-------|---------------------|----------|------|---------------|
| Adlestrop, Evenlode and Chastleton | 44 | Adlestrop | SP 241271 | 6 miles (9.7km) | 3 hrs | 571ft (174m) |
| Avon Valley | 66 | Saltford | ST 686673 | 7 miles (11.3km) | 3½ hrs | 755ft (230m) |
| Banbury, Oxford Canal and Broughton | 79 | Banbury Cross | SP 453403 | 10 miles (16km) | 4½ hrs | 469ft (143m) |
| Brockhampton, Sevenhampton and Whittington | 63 | East of Cheltenham | SP 010205 | 6½ miles (10.5km) | 3½ hrs | 853ft (260m) |
| Charlbury | 26 | Charlbury | SP 356194 | 6 miles (9.7km) | 3 hrs | 509ft (155m) |
| Chipping Campden and Broad Campden | 16 | Chipping Campden | SP 151391 | 3½ miles (5.6km) | 2 hrs | 525ft (160m) |
| Cirencester and the Duntisbourne Valley | 75 | Cirencester | SP 023020 | 8½ miles (13.7km) | 4½ hrs | 522ft (159m) |
| Crickley Hill and Leckhampton Hill | 60 | Crickley Hill Country Park | SO 930163 | 7 miles (11.3km) | 3½ hrs | 951ft (290m) |
| Deerhurst, Apperley and the River Severn | 49 | Deerhurst | SO 868298 | 7 miles (11.3km) | 3½ hrs | 164ft (50m) |
| Dursley, Uley and Owlpen | 87 | Dursley | ST 756981 | 8½ miles (13.7km) | 4½ hrs | 722ft (220m) |
| Edgeworth and Pinbury Park | 28 | Edgeworth | SO 945063 | 5½ miles (8.9km) | 3 hrs | 689ft (210m) |
| Frocester Hill and Nympsfield | 22 | Coaley Peak Picnic Site | SO 794014 | 4½ miles (7.2km) | 2½ hrs | 764ft (233m) |
| Lechlade, Kelmscott and the River Thames | 52 | Lechlade | SU 214995 | 7½ miles (12.1km) | 3½ hrs | 236ft (72m) |
| Longborough, Sezincote and Bourton-on-the-Hill | 32 | Longborough | SP 178296 | 5½ miles (8.9km) | 2½ hrs | 591ft (180m) |
| Macaroni Downs and the Leach Valley | 72 | Eastleach Turville | SP 198052 | 7½ miles (12.1km) | 4 hrs | 476ft (145m) |
| Malmesbury and the River Avon | 14 | Malmesbury, Old Station Yard | ST 932874 | 2 miles (3.2km) | 1 hr | 246ft (75m) |
| Milton under Wychwood and Fifield | 38 | Milton under Wychwood | SP 264183 | 6 miles (9.7km) | 3 hrs | 492ft (150m) |
| Miserden and Winstone | 30 | Miserden | SO 937088 | 5 miles (8km) | 2½ hrs | 804ft (245m) |
| Northleach and Farmington | 24 | Northleach | SP 113145 | 5 miles (8km) | 2½ hrs | 636ft (194m) |
| Painswick and the Beacon | 58 | Painswick | SO 865095 | 6 miles (9.7km) | 3 hrs | 928ft (283m) |
| Robins Wood Hill | 18 | Robinswood Hill Country Park | SO 838158 | 2½ miles (4km) | 1½ hrs | 650ft (198m) |
| Seven Springs and the Churn Valley | 41 | Seven Springs | SO 967170 | 6 miles (9.7km) | 3 hrs | 886ft (270m) |
| Sharpness and Berkeley | 46 | Sharpness | SO 667021 | 6½ miles (10.5km) | 3 hrs | 56ft (17m) |
| Sherborne and the River Windrush | 69 | Sherborne Park | SP 159143 | 7½ miles (12.1km) | 3½ hrs | 591ft (180m) |
| Somerford Keynes and the River Thames | 35 | Cotswold Water Park | SU 028959 | 6 miles (9.7km) | 3 hrs | 305ft (93m) |
| Stow-on-the-Wold, Broadwell and Donnington | 55 | Stow-on-the-Wold | SP 192258 | 6 miles (9.7km) | 3 hrs | 705ft (215m) |
| Tetbury and Westonbirt | 83 | Tetbury | ST 891931 | 9½ miles (15.3km) | 4½ hrs | 469ft (143m) |
| Thames and Severn Canal and Cerney Wick | 20 | Cotswold Water Park | SU 063962 | 4½ miles (7.2km) | 2½ hrs | 295ft (90m) |

## Comments

Both Adlestrop and Evenlode are delightful villages that overlook the Evenlode Valley, and the route passes by a splendid 17th-century manor house.

There are distant views of both Bath and Bristol from the higher points on this route, which also includes a stretch along a disused railway track and some pleasant riverside walking.

After an opening stretch along the towpath of the Oxford Canal, the route heads across fields to Broughton Castle before returning to Banbury.

A walk amidst the rolling wold country of the upper Coln Valley that takes in three villages and some fine views.

A fairly flat walk of wide and extensive views across the valley of the River Evenlode, including the wooded slopes of Wychwood Forest towards the end.

For much of this route the tower of Chipping Campden's famous 'wool church' is in sight.

The Duntisbourne Valley is followed from Cirencester, through Stratton, Daglingworth and on to the secluded and idyllic hamlet of Duntisbourne Rouse.

Both Crickley Hill and Leckhampton Hill occupy the Cotswold escarpment and provide outstanding views over Cheltenham and the Vale of Severn.

The two Saxon churches at Deerhurst are of great historic interest, and the walk ends with a lovely ramble beside the River Severn.

After an energetic opening stretch along the Cotswold escarpment between Dursley and Uley, the remainder of the walk is fairly flat, except for a final climb through woodland.

You pass a medieval church, two manor houses and make two descents into the thickly wooded valley of the River Frome.

The walk starts and finishes on the Cotswold escarpment, visits two prehistoric barrows and includes a climb through woodland.

Most of this flat walk in the upper Thames Valley between Lechlade and Kelmscott is across meadows, either close to or beside the river.

The walk links two attractive villages and passes close to an unusual country house, built to resemble an Indian palace.

Two beautiful, adjacent villages are at the start of this walk, which takes you through the valley of the little River Leach and onto the Macaroni Downs.

This short and easy walk mainly follows the meandering River Avon across meadows below the abbey town of Malmesbury.

There are some superb areas of woodland and wide views across the Evenlode Valley. The walk also passes close to a large country house.

Between Miserden and Winstone, the route descends into the well-wooded Frome Valley and passes through part of Misarden Park.

You can combine a fine scenic walk with a visit to the church at Northleach, one of the grandest of Cotswold 'wool churches'.

There are plenty of 'ups and downs' on this walk but none of them is particularly steep or strenuous. The views from Painswick Beacon are outstanding.

A short but fairly steep climb leads to a glorious viewpoint over the Cotswolds and the city of Gloucester.

From Seven Springs, the noise of the heavy traffic is soon left behind, and you pass through two quiet villages on this undemanding walk in the Churn Valley.

After heading inland from the Severn Estuary to Berkeley, you return to the river for a final stretch alongside the estuary. There are fine views of the Forest of Dean.

After descending through the woodlands of Sherborne Park into the village, the route continues first by Sherborne Brook and later by the River Windrush before returning to the start.

There are wide views across some of the lakes of the Cotswold Water Park, and part of the route is alongside the infant River Thames.

This walk in typical wold country starts and finishes in one of the most appealing of Cotswold towns.

A lengthy but generally flat walk which takes you from Tetbury to the superb woodlands of Westonbirt Arboretum.

A flat walk in the Cotswold Water Park that uses both a disused railway track and the towpath of a disused canal.

# *Introduction to*
# *More Cotswold Walks*

This second *Pathfinder* title on the Cotswolds covers the same area as the first title, except that this area is extended slightly westwards to include two walks in the Vale of Severn. This is to add greater variety to the selection of routes.

Nowhere else in the country do the work of nature and the work of man appear to be in greater harmony than in the Cotswolds. There are other parts of England that possess more dramatic scenery and there are equally attractive villages in other regions, but here is a combination of idyllic stone villages and small towns set amidst a gentle, rolling countryside that is without parallel and quintessentially 'English'.

How has this uniquely attractive combination been created and largely preserved? To explain this we need to examine three major factors relating to the geology, history and geography of the region: the local stone, the development of the woollen industry and the lack of nearby coal deposits.

### Local stone

The Cotswolds form part of a line of uplands, composed of oolitic limestone, that stretches in a roughly north-east to south-west direction from Yorkshire to Dorset. *Wold* is a Saxon word meaning 'upland'; the origin of *cot* is more difficult to establish. One theory is that it comes from the Saxon word for sheep enclosure; an alternative suggestion is that it is derived from *Cod*, the name of a Saxon chief who settled in the upper Windrush valley. Possibly the name Cotswold originally may have referred only to the area around the Windrush, later extended to cover the whole of this upland region.

Unlike the carboniferous limestone of the Yorkshire Dales and the Mendips, oolitic limestone does not create deep gorges and underground cave systems but a more intimate and less dramatic landscape characterised by rolling hills and gentle valleys. The Cotswolds tilt slightly to the south-east, thereby thrusting up a bold and often steep escarpment on their western edge. From this escarpment a succession of fine viewpoints – Dover's Hill, Broadway Tower, Cleeve Common, Cooper's Hill, Haresfield Beacon, Wotton Hill and Hinton Hill – look westwards over the lowlands of the vales of Evesham, Gloucester and Berkeley to the equally bold outlines of the Malverns, Shropshire Hills and Black Mountains on the distant horizon. Nearer at hand the eye is drawn to a number of individual outlying hills detached from the main Cotswold range; two of the most prominent of these are Bredon Hill near Evesham and Robins Wood Hill overlooking Gloucester.

Behind the escarpment lies the long 'dip' slope. Here is the typical rolling wold country which drops gently to the formerly extensive royal hunting ground of Wychwood Forest and merges almost imperceptibly into the flat country of the Oxford Plain. In the north of the region a number of rivers with delightful-sounding names – Evenlode, Windrush, Leach, Coln – have cut wide valleys through the wolds, flowing south-eastwards into the plain eventually to join the Thames, a Cotswold river in its origin. Only in the south, in the narrower valleys around Stroud, do the rivers flow westwards to the Severn.

Uniquely among Cotswold rivers, the Bristol Avon describes a great arc, flowing first eastwards, then turning southwards and finally curving westwards through Bradford-on-Avon and on to Bath, to form an obvious southern boundary to the Cotswolds. The northern edge is less clearly defined but here the line

*Eastleach Martin, Gloucestershire*

of limestone uplands descends to the valley of another River Avon, the Warwickshire or Shakespeare's Avon.

Cotswold stone makes excellent building material and has been used extensively for this purpose. One of its most appealing features is the variation in colour shades, which can range, depending on area, from light grey through pale cream, yellow, honey and deep golden to light brown. It is above all the quality and colour of this limestone, which invariably looks warm on even the dullest day, which makes the villages and small towns of the region so attractive. So well do some of the smaller villages blend into their natural surroundings that they seem to be an integral part of the landscape.

## Woollen industry

In his *Britannia,* published in 1610, William Camden says of the Cotswolds: 'In these Woulds there feed, in great numbers, flockes of sheepe'. If the local limestone produced the basic material for the buildings of the region, it was the prosperity generated initially by these 'flockes of sheepe' that provided the money for them. Much of the rich architectural heritage of the Cotswolds comes from the development of the medieval wool trade.

Sheep-farming began with the first human inhabitants of the region. With their dry slopes and sheltered valleys, the Cotswolds were a popular area for settlement from earliest times and a large number of varied prehistoric monuments survive. Among the best-known and most impressive of these are the burial chamber at Belas Knap, the group of remains known collectively as the Rollright Stones, and the Iron Age fortifications, which made use of the high vantage points. The summits of Bredon Hill, Cleeve Hill and Haresfield Beacon are among many that are crowned with such defensive earthworks but the most elaborate and extensive are those that occupy the plateau of Minchinhampton Common above the Frome and Nailsworth valleys.

The Romans found the area congenial and relatively easy to penetrate. They established Corinium (Cirencester) as one of their principal cities and Aquae Sulis (Bath) as their major health resort, building a number of villas, for

example at Chedworth and Witcombe, and constructing a series of roads – Foss Way, Ermin Street, Akeman Street – across the region. After the Romans came the Anglo-Saxons, who founded most of the present-day settlements and later introduced Christianity. Last in the line of conquerors were the Normans, who in the years after 1066 rebuilt

*Cotswold Water Park, near Cerney Wick, Gloucestershire*

many of the churches, established strong castles on the fringes of the region at Oxford and Gloucester and also created the royal forest of Wychwood, which lies around Burford, Charlbury and Woodstock.

It was the monastic foundations of the Cotswolds (Cirencester, Winchcombe, Hailes) that helped to pioneer the development of the wool trade, which reached its peak between the 14th and 17th centuries. At first the raw wool was exported to the continent but in the early 14th century Edward III imported weavers from Flanders to develop a native cloth industry. Over the next few centuries the manufacturing of woollen cloth expanded and prospered and by the end of the Middle Ages it had become England's major export industry. Half of it was produced in the Cotswolds, where the advantages of an abundance of sheep, water power and good communications ensured the predominance of the region.

It is from this heyday of the cloth trade that the distinguished architectural legacy of the area – domestic, commercial and religious – chiefly dates. This includes comparatively humble buildings, like small village churches, farm-houses, market halls and the modest but dignified houses and cottages that adorn such delightful places as Castle Combe, Bourton-on-the-Water and Bibury, as well as the grander town houses of wool merchants and the manor houses at Minster Lovell, Snowshill and Chastleton. Particularly outstanding are the magnificent 15th-century 'wool churches', endowed by wealthy wool magnates like William Grevel of Chipping Campden and the Forteys of Northleach. All visitors will have their favourites, but probably the most impressive are those that rise above Cirencester, Winchcombe, Burford, Chipping Campden and Northleach.

## Lack of coal

It is fortunate that much of this rich legacy has survived relatively intact and unspoilt and this is largely due to the absence of local coal deposits. With the onset of the Industrial Revolution, and in particular the application of first water- and later steam-powered machinery, the Cotswold woollen industry declined, unable to compete with the textile areas on the slopes of the Pennines, which had the advantages of faster-flowing streams and proximity to coal. Only the area around Stroud, where the streams are fast flowing, was able to expand and prolong its status as an important cloth-producing region into the early 19th century, until it also lost out to the more powerful woollen industries of Yorkshire. Here the narrow valleys, with their steep sides covered in tiers of houses and with 19th-century mills in the valley bottoms, rather resemble the Pennine valleys of Lancashire and Yorkshire – except that they never became extensively urbanised and industrialised.

Throughout the region the decline of the woollen industry led to much hardship and poverty – it is difficult to conceive of such an obviously prosperous area as this ever suffering hardship – but paradoxically it was this that was largely instrumental in preserving the attractiveness of the Cotswolds. Relative economic stagnation prevented the large-scale rebuilding, urbanisation and inevitable environmental damage that scarred so many other parts of Britain during the era of the Industrial Revolution.

In time a regeneration took place, largely based on the permanent advantages of the region – its climate, countryside and accessibility – that made it an attractive place to live and later a popular tourist area. A number of great country houses were built during the 18th and 19th centuries, including Cornbury Park, Blenheim Palace and Sezincote. In the late Georgian and Regency periods Cheltenham prospered and expanded as a fashionable spa and residential town. William Morris, the influential Victorian arbiter of taste and social reformer, helped to start off the tourist industry by popularising such beauty spots as Bibury and Broadway. During the 20th century the car has opened up the whole area to many more visitors and now tourism has become a vital part of the economy of the Cotswolds.

In Shakespeare's *Richard II* the Cotswolds are described as 'high wild hills and rough uneven ways', but in the main this is no longer true. Apart from a few remaining unenclosed 'wild' areas such as Cleeve Common, this is an intimate and largely tamed landscape where the man-made features of churches, villages, farms and manor houses fit snugly into their physical surroundings of hills and valleys, fields and woodlands. By far the best way to explore and appreciate at first hand this uniquely beautiful and harmonious corner of England is on foot and an extensive network of waymarked paths enables you to do that – an immensely rewarding and pleasurable experience.

# Malmesbury
# and the River Avon

| | |
|---|---|
| **Start** | Malmesbury, Old Station Yard car park |
| **Distance** | 2 miles (3.2km) |
| **Approximate time** | 1 hour |
| **Parking** | Old Station Yard car park at Malmesbury |
| **Refreshments** | Pubs and cafés at Malmesbury |
| **Ordnance Survey maps** | Landranger 173 (Swindon & Devizes), Explorer 168 (Stroud, Tetbury & Malmesbury) |

*Malmesbury occupies a hilltop site above the water meadows of the River Avon, and this short walk is across some of these meadows, following the various branches of the river around the edge of the town. It uses part of the Malmesbury Riverwalk, established by the local civic trust in the 1970s, which consists of a mixture of public and permissive footpaths, waymarked by green triangles. The succession of attractive views of the town are inevitably dominated by the still impressive ruins of its once great abbey.*

With your back to the river, turn right across the picnic area and by a road junction, keep ahead through a kissing-gate – Rotary Way signs here – and walk along a tree-lined path beside the river. Go through a kissing-gate and keep ahead to a road by the Duke of York pub **Ⓐ**.

Turn right to cross the bridge over the river, immediately turn left down steps, climb a stile and follow a path across meadows, bearing right to the corner. Climb two stiles in quick succession, bear left and head diagonally across the next meadow. Cross a footbridge, keep ahead to a road and turn right. The road (St John's Street) curves left to a T-junction by the old almshouses of St John's Hospital.

Turn left, cross the Avon by the imposing Avon Mills, former silk mills

built in the 1790s, and just after following the road round a right-hand bend, turn right through a gate **Ⓑ** onto a permissive path. Climb a stile, keep along the right-hand edge of a meadow and, after going through a kissing-gate, keep ahead to emerge briefly onto the right-hand edge of a sloping field. Continue into trees, cross two footbridges, go through a kissing-gate and walk across a meadow to another kissing-gate. Keep ahead alongside a hedge on the right, pass through a gap into the next meadow and turn right onto a paved path **Ⓒ**, first crossing a bridge over a minor channel and then turning right to cross the main river.

Walk along a walled tarmac path to a road and turn right – not along the road that leads into a new housing area but along a tarmac path (Burnivale) that

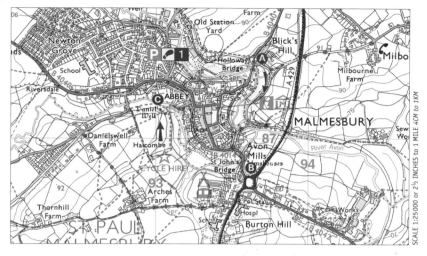

heads uphill. Turn left to ascend steps, bear right and continue up into the town centre of Malmesbury, a pleasant little town with a number of attractive streets and buildings. Although only about one-third of its original size, the Benedictine abbey, founded in the 7th century, is still a most imposing building. The present church, mainly comprising part of the nave, was built in the 12th century and is entered by a magnificent Norman porch. Inside is the tomb of the Saxon king Athelstan. Look out in the churchyard for an epitaph on a tombstone that records the unusual death of a woman in 1703, mauled by a tiger which had escaped from a travelling circus that had been visiting the town.

Turn left, passing to the left of the abbey, and just past the Old Bell Hotel turn right into Mill Lane. Head downhill, curving left to cross a bridge over the river, and turn left to return to the start. ●

*Malmesbury Abbey*

# *Chipping Campden and Broad Campden*

| | |
|---|---|
| **Start** | Chipping Campden |
| **Distance** | 3½ miles (5.6km) |
| **Approximate time** | 2 hours |
| **Parking** | Roadside parking at Chipping Campden |
| **Refreshments** | Pubs and cafés at Chipping Campden, pub at Broad Campden |
| **Ordnance Survey maps** | Landranger 151 (Stratford-upon-Avon), Explorer OL45 (The Cotswolds) |

*Most of this short and easy walk is across the meadows and fields that lie to the south of Chipping Campden, between this small town and the neighbouring village of Broad Campden. The highlights of the route are the many fine views across the fields of the tower of Chipping Campden's superb wool church.*

With its wealth of mellowed, grey and cream stone houses, 17th-century Market Hall and 15th-century church, Chipping Campden is the Cotswold wool town *par excellence.* Its dignified curving High Street is acclaimed as one of the finest in the country, a superb essay in harmony with diversity, with buildings of all ages from the 14th century onwards – but mostly a reflection of the town's prosperity in the 'golden age' of the Cotswold wool trade, in the later Middle Ages and on into the 16th and 17th centuries. The church is a magnificent example of a wool church, its Perpendicular tower dominating the town. Inside are monuments to

*Chipping Campden from the Coneygree*

some of Chipping Campden's wool merchants, including William Grevel, whose 14th-century house still stands in the High Street, and Sir Baptist Hicks, a 17th-century cloth merchant and first Viscount Campden (d. 1629), who was responsible for two of the town's most admired pieces of architecture: the delightful row of almshouses (1612) just below the church and the Market Hall (1627).

✏ Start by the Market Hall and walk along the main street towards the church. Take the first road on the right, which curves left to the church, and turn right along Station Road. At a public footpath sign – and a National Trust sign 'The Coneygree' – turn right Ⓐ over a stone stile and walk straight across the Coneygree, an area of meadowland bought by the National Trust to preserve the surroundings of the church.

Head downhill, at the bottom cross a footbridge, turn right and walk diagonally across a field. After crossing another footbridge, turn sharp left Ⓑ and head across the next field to climb a stile in the far corner. Continue across a field, go through a metal gate and, where the path divides, bear slightly right and head across to climb the right-hand one of the two stiles seen in front. Walk gently uphill across the next field, climb a stile on the far side, continue gently downhill across a field and pass through a hedge gap.

Bear right across a field, go through another gap and continue along the left-hand edge of the next field, by a brook on the left. In the field corner, turn left to cross the brook, go through a metal kissing-gate and head uphill along the right-hand field edge to a stile. Climb it, continue along a track, go through a gate and keep ahead to a narrow lane. Turn left, at a T-junction turn right Ⓒ through the picturesque village of Broad Campden, and the road heads downhill and bends right.

Where the road bends left in front of a chapel, keep ahead along a tarmac track Ⓓ, passing to the left of the chapel, and at a fork take the left-hand track – public footpath sign here to Chipping Campden – passing in front of a row of cottages. Where the track ends by an 18th-century Quaker meeting house, bear left along an enclosed path to a kissing-gate. Go through and continue along a path, crossing a drive in front of a large cottage. Go through another kissing-gate and keep ahead along the right-hand edge of a field. Ahead the houses and church tower of Chipping Campden come into view.

The path bears left to continue across the field, then keeps along its left-hand edge – parallel to a road – to reach a track. Turn left towards the road but immediately turn right along a tarmac track (George Lane) and follow it into Chipping Campden. Where the track ends, keep ahead in a straight line – first along a road, then between houses, and finally through a car park and under an arch – to emerge onto the main street just to the left of the Market Hall. ●

# Robins Wood Hill

| Start | Robinswood Hill Country Park, signposted from A38 on southern edge of Gloucester |
|---|---|
| Distance | 2½ miles (4km) |
| Approximate time | 1½ hours |
| Parking | Robinswood Hill Country Park, by the visitor centre |
| Refreshments | Light refreshments at visitor centre |
| Ordnance Survey maps | Landranger 162 (Gloucester & Forest of Dean), Explorer 179 (Gloucester, Cheltenham & Stroud) |

*Robins Wood Hill is a westerly outlier of the Cotswolds and overlooks the city of Gloucester. Using a variety of colour-coded trails, you start from the base, head up through woodland and across open grassland to its summit – 651ft (198m) high – and then descend back to the start. Although only a short walk, the climb is quite a steep one, but from the summit ridge you enjoy extensive and contrasting views: along the Cotswold ridge in one direction and over Gloucester – inevitably dominated by the cathedral – in the other. The multitude of paths in the country park can be confusing but the different trails are well signed, and if you do stray off the suggested route, it is easy to make your way back to the start by simply heading downhill in the direction of the cathedral tower.*

Robinswood Hill Country Park, which occupies about two-thirds of the hill, was created in 1974 as a recreational amenity for the people of Gloucester. At a tree trunk by the visitor centre – where the walk begins – all the various colour-coded trails are shown, and you start by taking the yellow trail.

With your back to the visitor centre entrance, turn left up steps and immediately turn left along a grassy path. At a fork by a yellow post, bear left into the trees and on meeting a clear stony path, bear left again. At the next fork, take the left-hand, tree-lined path along the edge of the country park and look out for where a yellow post

directs you to turn right. Cross a footbridge to a T-junction, turn right gently uphill through woodland, bearing first left and then right to a junction. Turn half-left to reach a tarmac path, cross it, keep ahead to cross another path and continue uphill.

Cross another path – following the yellow trail all the while – and keep ahead up a long flight of steps through dense woodland. Bear right on joining another path and continue more gently uphill to a T-junction. Turn left, pass beside a fence and at a crossing of paths, turn right. Continue along the left-hand path at a fork – now on both yellow and white trails – and head up over more open country to the brow of the hill **A**. Turn right here onto a dark green trail, ascend steps and continue along the summit ridge to the triangulation pillar. The extensive views from here take in Gloucester Cathedral, the Vale of Severn, Forest of Dean and the western edge of the Cotswolds.

Continue along this superb ridge path, later descending steeply. Keep ahead at a crossing of paths and continue down to a junction of paths by a footpath post **B**. Turn right – joining the blue trail – descend to a T-junction and turn right again along a track. The track heads gently downhill, enters woodland and then emerges into more open country, from where there is a particularly impressive view over the city of Gloucester.

*The Cotswold escarpment from Robins Wood Hill*

The track then curves right into woodland again and at a T-junction, turn left downhill. Take the left-hand, grassy path at a fork and continue down over several crossings of paths back to the visitor centre. ●

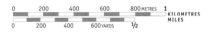

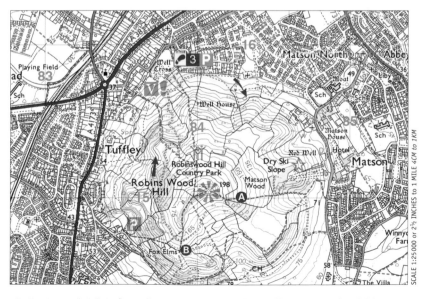

# Thames and Severn Canal and Cerney Wick

| | |
|---|---|
| **Start** | Cotswold Water Park, Bridge car park |
| **Distance** | 4½ miles (7.2km) |
| **Approximate time** | 2½ hours |
| **Parking** | Bridge car park |
| **Refreshments** | Pub at Cerney Wick |
| **Ordnance Survey maps** | Landranger 163 (Cheltenham & Cirencester), Explorer 169 (Cirencester & Swindon) |

*The track of a disused railway and the towpath of a disused canal are utilised to create an attractive and absorbing walk in the Cotswold Water Park. There is some superb woodland, fine views across lakes and the historic interest provided by abandoned railway bridges and canal locks.*

The fine brick arches of a disused railway bridge in the car park is an indication that the first part of the walk is along a disused railway track, formerly part of the Midland Junction Railway, which ran between Cheltenham and Southampton. Since closure in the 1960s, it has been converted into a footpath and cycleway.

🖉 Begin by going through a gate in the corner of the car park, at a public footpath sign to South Cerney and Lakes, and walk along an enclosed, hedge-lined track, passing between lakes both sides. The track emerges, via a gate, onto a road. Turn left and, where the road curves left into South Cerney, turn sharp right through a gate **Ⓐ** and walk along an enclosed path. The path bends left to pass under a disused bridge, bends right beside the brick arches and turns left at a fence corner to continue in a straight line, between garden fences on the left and woodland on the right. After briefly emerging by

the side of a road, the path continues along the right-hand edge of a playing field, crosses the River Churn and keeps ahead along a lovely tree-lined avenue to pass under the brick arches of another disused railway bridge.

Immediately turn left beside the bridge, cross a plank footbridge and climb steps, bending left up to a lane. Turn left to cross the bridge **Ⓑ**, walk along the narrow lane as far as a public footpath sign to Cerney Wick and turn right along a hedge-lined track. On the left is the bed of the disused Thames and Severn Canal, built between 1783 and 1789 to link the two great river systems. It was never commercially successful and was finally abandoned in the 1920s, although stretches of it are currently being restored. Where the track turns right to a farm, keep ahead to climb a stile and continue along another lovely tree-lined path – still by the disused canal – to eventually reach a stile by a former lock in front of a

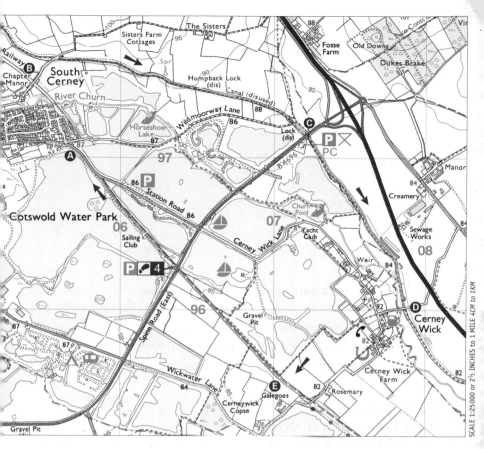

```
0      200    400    600    800 METRES   1
                                         KILOMETRES
                                         MILES
0      200    400    600 YARDS    ½
```

bridge. Climb it, keep ahead to climb another, cross a footbridge and climb steps up to a road **C**. Cross over, descend steps opposite, at a public footpath sign to Cerney Wick, climb a stile and keep ahead along a path signposted 'Lakeside Walk'. Continue by the left-hand edge of a lake and at the far end bear left in the corner of a meadow to enter woodland. Cross a footbridge and turn right to continue beside the dried-up bed of the canal. After passing the 18th-century Round House on the other side of the canal – built for employees of the canal company – the path reaches a lane **D**. Turn right into Cerney Wick, at a T-junction by the Crown Inn keep ahead over a stile, walk along the left field edge and climb a stile in the corner onto a narrow lane.

Climb the stile opposite, walk along the right-hand edge of a field, climb another stile and keep ahead along a wooden walkway, continuing along the left-hand edge of a meadow beside a lake. Turn right in the corner to continue along the edge of the meadow, turn left at a hedge corner, keep beside the lake and in the next corner, where the track bends right, turn left by a waymarked post and descend steps into trees.

Cross a footbridge, walk along the left-hand edge of a meadow, climb a stile in the corner and turn right, at a public footpath sign to South Cerney and Ashford Keynes, to rejoin the disused railway track **E**. Follow it for just over ½ mile (800m) back to the start. ●

# Frocester Hill and Nympsfield

| | |
|---|---|
| **Start** | Coaley Peak Picnic Site, off B4066 between Stroud and Dursley |
| **Distance** | 4½ miles (7.2km) |
| **Approximate time** | 2½ hours |
| **Parking** | Coaley Peak Picnic Site |
| **Refreshments** | Pub at Nympsfield |
| **Ordnance Survey maps** | Landranger 162 (Gloucester & Forest of Dean), Explorer 168 (Stroud, Tetbury & Malmesbury) |

*There is a strong prehistoric theme to this walk as it passes two neolithic long barrows, both situated on the Cotswold escarpment. The views from the escarpment on Frocester Hill, looking across to the Severn Estuary and the wooded hills of the Forest of Dean, are superb. The route descends from the hill to the village of Nympsfield and returns to it by a climb through attractive woodland.*

First make your way across the open grassland of the picnic site on Frocester Hill to Nympsfield Long Barrow. This neolithic burial chamber was built nearly 5,000 years ago and originally had a roof of limestone slabs. The remains of over 17 people have been found here.

Turn left at a waymarked post in front of the barrow and walk along the top of the escarpment to a kissing-gate. Go through – here entering the National Trust's Coaley Peak property – and keep ahead to the view-indicator which, at a height of 764ft (233m), gives tremendous views along the escarpment and

*Nympsfield Long Barrow*

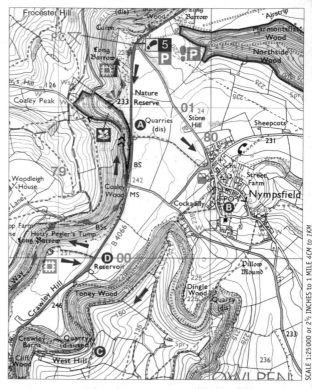

across the Vale of Berkeley below to the Severn Estuary and the Forest of Dean on the other side. At the view-indicator, turn left along a path that contours across the top slopes of the open, grassy hillside and at a fork take the left-hand, upper path, which climbs steadily to emerge onto a road at the top.

Turn right, at a public footpath sign turn left **A** over a stile and walk along a right-hand field edge. Go through a gate in the corner and continue along the left edge of the next field to a lane. Turn left and at a T-junction, turn right into Nympsfield. At a fork in front of the Rose and Crown, take the right-hand lane and about 100 yds (91m) before reaching the church – mostly 19th-century apart from the Perpendicular tower – turn right over a stone stile **B**. Head gently uphill and climb a stone stile in the top right-hand corner of the field onto a road.

Climb the stile opposite, head downhill across grass and follow a path into trees to a stile. Climb it, continue quite steeply downhill through woodland and at the bottom, keep ahead by the left inside edge of the trees. The path ascends to a crossroads where you turn left downhill, continuing along the left inside edge of the wood again. At a fork, take the left-hand lower path – by a wire fence on the left – and at a junction of paths by a stile on the left, turn sharp right **C** and head steeply uphill. Bear right on joining another path and continue less steeply up, finally curving left beside a metal gate onto the road.

Turn right and at a sign to Uley Long Barrow, turn left **D** onto a path that keeps along the right-hand edge of a field to the barrow. Nicknamed Hetty Pegler's Tump, this prehistoric burial mound is around the same age as the one at the start of the walk. It is about 180ft (55m) long and comprises a stone-built central passage with two chambers either side and a third one at the end.

Return to the road **D**, turn left and at a fork take the left-hand road, sign-posted to Frocester and Eastington. The road heads downhill. At a Cotswold Way sign, bear right onto a path into woodland, which descends, via a series of steps, passes below quarry faces and emerges onto the open grassland of Frocester Hill. Continue across the hillside to rejoin the outward route and retrace your steps to the start. ●

# Northleach and Farmington

| | |
|---|---|
| Start | Northleach |
| Distance | 5 miles (8km) |
| Approximate time | 2½ hours |
| Parking | Northleach, Market Place |
| Refreshments | Pubs and cafés at Northleach |
| Ordnance Survey maps | Landranger 163 (Cheltenham & Cirencester), Explorer OL45 (The Cotswolds) |

*This walk in the Leach Valley takes you along a mixture of lanes, field paths and tracks between Northleach and the hilltop village of Farmington. There are extensive views across rolling wold country, and the tower of the famous 'wool church' at Northleach is in sight for much of the final ¹/₂ mile (800m).*

The 15th-century church at Northleach, with its magnificent south porch, is acclaimed as one of the grandest among the many grand 'wool churches' of the Cotswolds, its imposing Perpendicular tower dominating the streets of the attractive small town. It reflects the heyday of the wool trade; inside are many monuments to the great wool merchants who created the town's prosperity. Handsome stone and half-timbered buildings line the High Street, and the inns are a reminder of Northleach's importance in the days of coach travel.

🖊 Start in the Market Place, then on the far side of the main street, take the wide tarmac path between houses, called Doctors Lane. On emerging onto a road, turn half-right, head up between houses to a T-junction and continue uphill along an enclosed path – later through woodland – to a lane **Ⓐ**. Turn left along the lane, passing under the A40, for

¾ mile (1.2km) and, where it bends left downhill, bear right onto a track **Ⓑ**.

After going through a metal gate, bear left and head gently downhill across a field, keeping more or less in line with a line of telegraph poles and aiming not for the first but the second waymarked footbridge below. Cross it, bear right and continue quite steeply uphill in the same direction as before to a waymarked stile on the ridge. Climb it, continue across the next field, climb a stile in the corner and keep ahead along a track, passing to the right of Farmington church to a lane **Ⓒ**. The

*Farmington church*

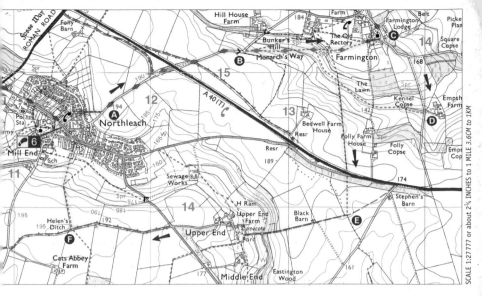

SCALE 1:27777 or about 2½ INCHES to 1 MILE 3.6CM to 1KM

| 0 | 200 | 400 | 600 | 800 METRES | 1 |
|---|-----|-----|-----|-----|---|
| | | | | | KILOMETRES |
| | | | | | MILES |
| 0 | 200 | 400 | 600 YARDS | ½ | |

village is to the left, centred around a large green and containing some handsome houses. The church is mainly Norman, with a Perpendicular tower.

The route continues to the right. Take the first lane on the right, signposted to Northleach and Burford, heading downhill, and in the dip turn right through a gate **D** at a public footpath sign, and walk across a field, parallel to a tiny brook on the right. Go through a gate, turn right to cross the brook, turn left and walk across a field. Cross a track, continue across the next field and, just before reaching the far side, turn half-right up to a waymarked gate. Go through, turn left along the left-hand field edge, climb a stile and continue along the left-hand field edge. Pass through a hedge gap in the corner, walk gently uphill along the left-hand edge of the next field and go through a gate onto the A40.

Carefully cross both the main road and a side road and follow a path through a gap in the trees to a stile. Climb it, keep ahead through woodland, climb another stile and continue straight across a field. Turn right through a metal gate **E** on the far side, keep along the right-hand edge of the next

two fields and then continue along an enclosed, tree-lined track. Go through a metal gate, head downhill along a track – passing to the left of a pool and crossing a footbridge over the outlet stream – keep ahead uphill and look out for where you turn right through a gate. Walk across a field and at a wall corner, turn left and continue up towards a large house. In the field corner go through a gate onto a lane and follow it to a T-junction.

Keep ahead along an enclosed track and after ½ mile (800m), turn right **F** at a public footpath sign, along the left-hand edge of a field, heading gently downhill. There is a superb view ahead over Northleach, dominated by its church tower. Climb a stile, continue downhill and, in the bottom corner, turn left through a gate and turn right to pass between tennis courts on the left and a children's play area on the right. At the corner of the tennis courts, bear left to cross a footbridge over the infant River Leach and keep ahead along an enclosed tarmac path to a road. Turn left back to the Market Place. ●

# Charlbury

| | |
|---:|:---|
| **Start** | Charlbury |
| **Distance** | 6 miles (9.7km) |
| **Approximate time** | 3 hours |
| **Parking** | Charlbury, Spendlove Centre |
| **Refreshments** | Pubs and café at Charlbury |
| **Ordnance Survey maps** | Landranger 164 (Oxford), Explorer 180 (Oxford) |

*This is an undemanding walk, mostly along well-defined paths and broad tracks, in the gently undulating countryside of the Evenlode Valley to the east and south of Charlbury. There are a series of extensive views, especially on the latter stages of the route, looking across the valley to Cornbury Park and the wooded slopes of Wychwood Forest.*

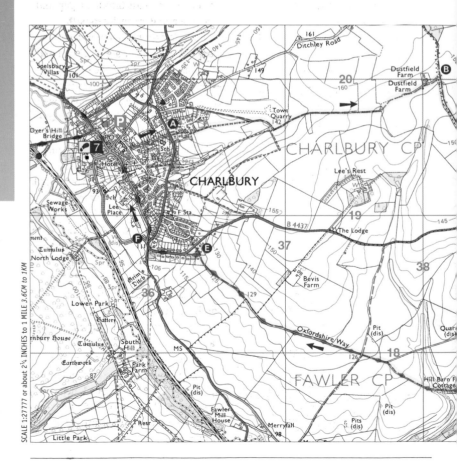

SCALE 1:27777 or about 2¼ INCHES to 1 MILE 3.6CM to 1KM

The quiet, pleasant little town of Charlbury has a fine situation on the eastern slopes of the Evenlode Valley, overlooking the wooded expanses of Wychwood Forest on the western slopes. It was once noted for its glove-making industry and has a number of old houses dating back to the 16th and 17th centuries. Dominating the town is the tower of its medieval church.

✐ Start in the town centre at the junction of Market Street, Church Street and Sheep Street and, facing the Bull Inn, take the road to the left of it (Browns Lane). Take the first turning on the right along the right-hand edge of a green, turn left at the end of the green and turn right along a track between houses. Cross a road **A**, continue along the tarmac track opposite, at a public footpath sign Centenary Woodland cross another road and walk along a tarmac path to a metal kissing-gate.

Go through, turn right through a hedge gap, turn left along the left-hand field edge and, where the hedge on the left finishes, continue straight ahead along a broad, grassy swathe. At its far, narrow end, keep ahead through another metal kissing-gate and, at the T-junction immediately in front, turn right along a tree- and hedge-lined path. Follow it around a left-hand bend and, on emerging from the trees, turn left along a track. Follow this track around a right-hand bend and continue to a T-junction just beyond a farmhouse **B**.

Turn sharp right along a track – initially along the left-hand field edge and later enclosed – which emerges onto a road. Cross over and take the path opposite along the right-hand edge of a field. In the corner, turn right **C** in front of a gate, pass through a gap and continue along an enclosed path. Follow this path in a more or less straight line – sometimes enclosed and sometimes along either the left- or right-hand edges of fields – as far as a crossroads. All the way there are extensive views across fields and the village seen over to the left is Stonesfield.

At the crossroads, turn right along a tarmac track **D**, here joining the Oxfordshire Way. Where the track bends right by a cottage, turn first left and then almost immediately right through a blue-waymarked gate. Keep along the left-hand field edge, go through a gate and continue along an undulating track. At a blue-waymarked post, the track narrows to a path, and you continue along this attractive, tree-lined path, eventually emerging onto a track **E**.

Turn left down to a road and keep ahead, following the road around a right-hand bend. At the bend, bear left along Hixet Wood **F**, head first down-hill and then continue up into Charlbury town centre. ●

# Edgeworth and Pinbury Park

| | |
|---|---|
| **Start** | Edgeworth, at top of lane leading to Edgeworth church |
| **Distance** | 5½ miles (8.9km) |
| **Approximate time** | 3 hours |
| **Parking** | Roadside parking at top of lane signposted to Edgeworth church |
| **Refreshments** | None |
| **Ordnance Survey maps** | Landranger 163 (Cheltenham & Cirencester), Explorer 168 (Stroud, Tetbury & Malmesbury) |

*This pleasant route does a circuit around the deep and well-wooded Frome Valley, descending and ascending to cross the small river twice. There is a particularly attractive stretch through Pinbury Park, passing in front of the house from where there are fine views across the valley, and some outstanding views near the end of the walk of Edgeworth Manor and church.*

Start by walking down the winding, undulating lane to the medieval church, which retains a fine Norman chancel and south doorway **Ⓐ**. Keep ahead along the drive towards

*View of the Frome Valley near Edgeworth*

Edgeworth Manor – built in the 17th century and enlarged in the 19th century – and in front of the gates, turn right onto a track that curves left and heads downhill, passing to the right of the house and continuing across part of the gardens and into woodland.

In front of a metal gate, turn right over a stile, keep ahead and then bear left to cross a bridge over the narrow River Frome. After going through a gate, the path heads uphill through trees to a lane. Turn right as far as a crossroads, turn right, in the Sapperton and Stroud direction, and at a public bridleway sign, turn left **Ⓑ** and walk along the left-hand

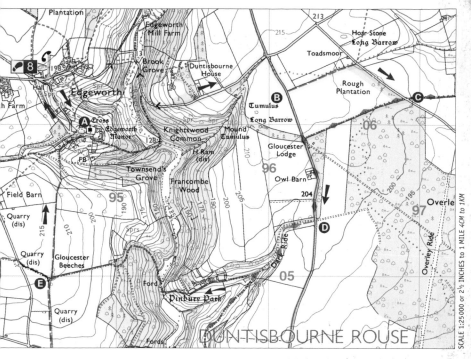

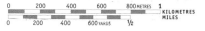

edge of a field. In the corner, follow a path through trees to a narrow lane, turn right and after ¼ mile (400km), turn right beside a gate **C**. Walk along a track through trees, continue along a left-hand field edge and go through a metal gate onto a lane.

Turn left, at a public bridleway sign turn right onto the grass verge and immediately turn right through a gate **D**. Make sure that you go through the gate on the right and not the one in front. Turn left alongside a hedge, parallel to the drive to Pinbury Park. After following the curve of the hedge to the left, veer away from it to continue just above the drive. At a small pool, join the drive and keep along it to where it bears right to Pinbury Park. Here continue downhill along a track, passing in front of the fine manor house, and to the left is a grand view over the deep and thickly wooded Frome Valley.

The track curves right into trees. Ignoring a path that branches off to the left, continue down to cross the river

again and go through a gate. Keep ahead through another one and head uphill through woodland, eventually emerging from the trees to reach a metal gate. After going through it, continue along the right-hand edge of two fields and in the corner of the second field – by a group of trees known as the Gloucester Beeches – go through a metal gate and immediately turn right through another gate **E**.

Keep along the right-hand edge of two fields. From this open, elevated position there are fine and extensive views all round, especially looking ahead to Edgeworth Manor and church. Continue downhill across a field into a hollow, keep ahead to the far side and turn right along a track. Go through a gate, continue along a tarmac drive, passing in front of cottages, to the church **A** and turn left to retrace your steps up the lane to the start.  ●

*Miserden and Winstone*

# Miserden and Winstone

| | |
|---|---|
| **Start** | Miserden |
| **Distance** | 5 miles (8km) |
| **Approximate time** | 2½ hours |
| **Parking** | Roadside parking at Miserden |
| **Refreshments** | Pub at Miserden |
| **Ordnance Survey maps** | Landranger 163 (Cheltenham & Cirencester), Explorer 179 (Gloucester, Cheltenham & Stroud) |

*The small and secluded villages of Miserden and Winstone occupy opposite sides of the thickly wooded and steep-sided Frome Valley, and this walk links them via field and woodland paths, going through part of Misarden Park. Both villages have interesting churches, and there are fine views across the valley.*

The walk starts in the centre of the pleasant village of Miserden, at the octagonal shelter built around a large tree. Nearby is the medieval church – much restored in the Victorian era –

*Miserden*

and the Carpenters Arms.

🔾 With your back to the pub, take the lane ahead and almost immediately turn right, at a public footpath sign, onto a path. The path soon bears left to continue as an enclosed path to a stone stile. Climb it, walk along a shady enclosed track and climb another stone stile onto a lane.

Turn left and, where the lane bears right, turn left through a kissing-gate **A** and head downhill across a field. As you descend there are fine views to the left across the Frome Valley, with Misarden Abbey clearly visible. This Jacobean mansion was restored in the 19th century and partly rebuilt by Lutyens in the 1920s following a fire. It is surrounded by fine gardens and parkland, and the gardens are open to the public in the summer on three days a week.

Go through another kissing-gate and continue downhill along the left, inside edge of woodland to reach a tarmac track. Turn left – still downhill – and at the bottom, turn right onto a track that bears right and continues alongside Misarden Park Lake. Now head uphill through woodland, curving right to join a tarmac drive at a bend and by a blue-waymarked post **B**. Walk along this beautiful, tree-lined drive to emerge through gates beside a lodge onto a lane.

Take the narrow lane opposite, turn left at a T-junction, in the Winstone and Birdlip direction, and the lane bends right **C** into the scattered village of Winstone. At a fork, take the left-hand, upper lane, signposted to Elkstone and Birdlip, which bends right, keep ahead at a crossroads, and at a public footpath sign turn right onto a tarmac track **D**. The track heads gently downhill to a lane, where you turn left for a brief detour to Winstone church, in an isolated and idyllic setting on the eastern edge of the village. This attractive building with a saddleback

tower dates back to around the Norman Conquest.

From the church, walk back along the lane back into the village. At a fork take the left-hand, lower lane and, at a public footpath sign, turn left onto a path **E** and head down to climb a stile. Walk across a field, go through a gate in the corner, bear right and head diagonally across the next field to climb a stile in the far corner onto a lane. Turn left and at a yellow-waymarked post, turn right along a track **F**. The track passes by farm buildings and continues in a straight line across fields, later bending right to keep along the left-hand edge of a field.

In the field corner, follow the track into woodland and, at a waymarked post, bear right and continue through this delightful woodland to a T-junction just to the left of the tarmac drive that was walked along earlier **B**. Turn left to rejoin the outward route and retrace your steps to the start, enjoying more grand views over the Frome Valley. ●

# Longborough, Sezincote and Bourton-on-the-Hill

| | |
|---|---|
| **Start** | Longborough |
| **Distance** | 5½ miles (8.9km) |
| **Approximate time** | 2½ hours |
| **Parking** | Roadside parking at Longborough |
| **Refreshments** | Pub at Longborough, pub at Bourton-on-the-Hill |
| **Ordnance Survey maps** | Landrangers 151 (Stratford-upon-Avon) and 163 (Cheltenham & Cirencester), Explorer OL45 (The Cotswolds) |

*From Longborough, this undemanding route heads in an almost straight line to Bourton-on-the-Hill, passing close to the impressive and unusual Sezincote House, built in an Oriental style. The return leg takes a more circuitous route across fields. Throughout the walk, there are fine views over the surrounding countryside of the north Cotswolds.*

Longborough is a pleasant and unpretentious village with attractive cottages and a medieval church that has a Norman doorway and 13th-century tower. Inside the church there are some interesting monuments.

The walk starts in the village centre by the war memorial and Coach and Horses. With your back to the pub and facing the church, turn left and, at a public footpath sign to Sezincote and Bourton-on-the-Hill, turn right along a tarmac track, which narrows to a path and leads to a gate.

Go through the gate, walk along the right-hand edge of a field, go through another gate and continue along the right-hand edge of fields. After passing through a belt of trees and through another gate, keep along the left-hand edge of the next field and cross a tarmac drive to a kissing-gate. Go through and walk initially along the left-hand field edge, by woodland on

the left, later bearing right and heading downhill towards a lake. Go through a gate at the bottom. As you continue across a field there is a grand view to the left of Sezincote House, built around the beginning of the 19th century for Charles Cockerell, a former employee of the East India Company, in an Indian design. At that time anything Oriental – Indian or Chinese – was highly fashionable. A Moghul palace set amidst landscaped English gardens and with a Cotswold backcloth is a strange sight, but it all seems to blend together beautifully.

Go through a gate **Ⓐ** across the end of an arm of the lake, go through another gate and continue by the right-hand field edge. At a fence corner, keep straight ahead across the field – crossing a tarmac drive – go through a kissing-gate on the far side, keep ahead to go through another and continue across the next field. The houses and

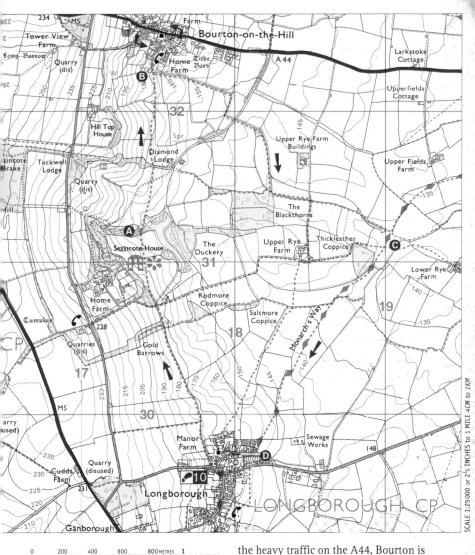

| 0 | 200 | 400 | 600 | 800 METRES | 1 |
|---|---|---|---|---|---|
| | | | | | KILOMETRES |
| | | | | | MILES |
| 0 | 200 | 400 | 600 YARDS | ½ | |

church tower of Bourton-on-the-Hill can be seen ahead. Climb a stile, keep ahead across the next two fields, going through two gates, and then continue along the left-hand edge of the next field to point **B**. Go through another gate and walk along an enclosed path to a lane.

Turn right for a short circuit of Bourton-on-the-Hill. Follow the lane around a left-hand bend to the main road and turn left uphill, passing the mainly 15th-century church. Despite the heavy traffic on the A44, Bourton is still an attractive village with some fine 17th- and 18th-century cottages. Take the first lane on the left, at a T-junction turn left downhill and, at a public footpath sign to Sezincote and Longborough, turn right onto a path and retrace your steps back to the second gate **B**.

After going through it, turn left along the left-hand field edge, go through a gate and keep along the left-hand edge of the next three fields, going through two more gates. On reaching a wide hedge gap, turn right, in the direction of a yellow waymark, along an enclosed,

*Longborough*

hedge-lined path and, at the next way-marked post, turn left along the left-hand field edge and climb a stile onto a tarmac drive. Climb the stile opposite, keep along the left-hand field edge, climb a stile in the corner and keep ahead along a narrow path through trees to climb another stile.

Continue along the left-hand edge of the next field and in the corner turn left over a footbridge. Keep by the right-hand field edge to a stile. Climb it, turn right through a gate beside a cattle-grid and walk along a tarmac track, going through another gate, towards a farm. Where the track turns right, keep ahead in front of a house and beside a barn to a T-junction. Turn left, go through a gate and continue along a wide, grassy path across fields, curving left to go through a gate at a corner of a wood. Turn right initially along the left-hand edge of the trees, continue across the field but at a crossing of paths about half-way across – not easy to spot –

turn right **C**, head across towards the wood again and go through a gate in the field corner.

Walk along the right-hand edge of the next field, looking out for yellow waymarks in the fence on the right where you turn half-left and head across to another waymark on the far side. Turn right to continue along the left-hand field edge, curving left to cross a footbridge, and bear right across the corner of a field to a stile. Climb it, keep in the same direction across the next field towards Longborough church, cross a footbridge over a ditch and bear left diagonally across a field to a stile in the far corner.

Climb the stile, keep along the right-hand field edge but almost immediately turn right over a stile and bear left across the next field towards houses on the edge of Longborough. Climb a stile on the far side, walk along an enclosed tarmac path to a road and keep ahead to a T-junction **D**. Turn right through the village and turn left by the church to return to the start. ●

# Somerford Keynes and the River Thames

| | |
|---|---|
| **Start** | Cotswold Water Park, Keynes Country Park |
| **Distance** | 6 miles (9.7km) |
| **Approximate time** | 3 hours |
| **Parking** | Keynes Country Park, near lakeside café |
| **Refreshments** | Café at Country Park, pub at Somerford Keynes |
| **Ordnance Survey maps** | Landranger 163 (Cheltenham & Cirencester), Explorer 169 (Cirencester & Swindon) |

*This is the second walk in this guide in the Cotswold Water Park. It is a flat and easy route which starts by heading across to the village of Somerford Keynes and then follows a stretch of the Thames Path – at this stage the river is nothing more than a narrow stream. There are many extensive views across the numerous lakes that make up the Water Park and a particularly attractive and relaxing finale along a tree-lined lakeside path.*

Keynes Country Park is in the heart of the Cotswold Water Park, an extensive area of lakes in the upper Thames Valley – over 130 and still growing – created from gravel extraction. It has become an established and popular centre for watersports of all kinds, plus other outdoor activities: cycling, horse-riding and walking.

🖊 The walk begins by the lakeside café. Turn left along the tarmac drive back towards the entrance to the country park and, at a T-junction, turn right onto a track that keeps along the left-hand edge of a lake. Where the track ends, bear right across grass, pass through a fence gap and turn sharp left over a stile **Ⓐ**.

Walk along a path that turns right, continue between a hedge on the left and the embankment of current gravel workings on the right, and climb a stile in a hedge. Follow the path to the left, along the left, inside edge of woodland,

climb a stile and keep ahead across a field, keeping parallel to its right-hand edge. After crossing a footbridge, keep ahead in the same direction across the next field and climb a stile onto a lane. Cross over, climb the stile opposite, at a public footpath sign to Somerford Keynes, and turn right onto a narrow path that runs through a belt of woodland parallel to the lane. The path bends left – still parallel with the lane – and briefly emerges onto the edge of a field, turning right to a stile.

Climb it to rejoin the lane, turn left and follow the lane into Somerford Keynes. On the edge of the village, turn right along a lane signposted to 'Parish Church' **Ⓑ** and turn left over a stone stile, at a public footpath sign. Walk along an enclosed path, turn right towards the medieval church at a T-junction in front of a wall and bear left through a kissing-gate at a public

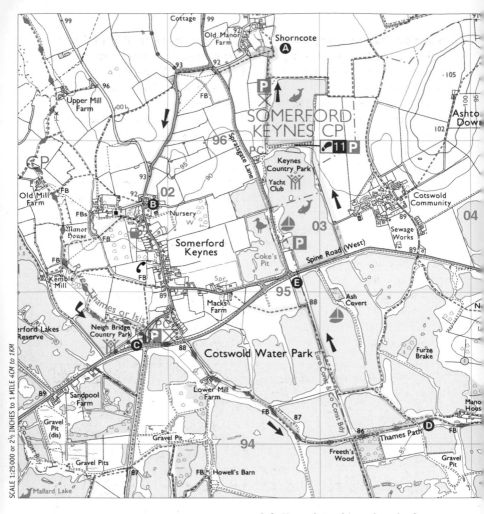

SCALE 1:25000 or 2½ INCHES to 1 MILE 4CM to 1KM

footpath sign to Oaksey Moor. Head diagonally across a field, cross a footbridge on the far side, walk initially along the right-hand edge of the next field and then continue straight across it. On the far side, turn left along the field edge, here joining the Thames Path, and turn right through a kissing-gate in the corner.

Keep along the right-hand edge of the next field – the infant River Thames is over to the right – and in the corner, cross a footbridge over the river and turn left onto a tree-lined path, between a lake on the right and the river on the left. Keep along this path and, after emerging from the trees, bear left across to the corner of a meadow to re-enter woodland and continue along a path that bends right to reach a road by Neigh Bridge Country Park car park **C**. Turn left to cross a bridge over the Thames and, where the road bends left back into Somerford Keynes, turn right along Mill Lane.

Cross a main road, continue along the lane opposite. After passing a farmhouse, the lane continues as a broad track between lakes. At a Thames Path marker-post in front of gates, turn right to cross a footbridge over the river and follow the path to the left to continue between the river on the left and a lake on the right. This attractive path later continues through woodland, and you keep along it as far as a footbridge and public footpath sign.

Turn left ❶ to cross the footbridge over the Thames – here leaving the Thames Path – climb a stile and continue by the right-hand edge of a lake, between trees on the left and a wire fence on the right. On emerging onto a broad track, turn left along a causeway between two lakes, follow the track around a right-hand bend and continue as far as a waymarked post. Turn left here through a hedge gap and turn right to continue along a lakeside path which later widens into a track. Follow this track to the left around the

end of the lake and about 20 yds (18m) after emerging into rough, open grassland, bear left off the track onto a narrow, faint but discernible path – not easy to spot initially – which continues in a straight line to a waymarked post.

Cross a track, keep ahead along a faint path and climb a stile in a hedge onto the main road. Turn right and, just beyond a large notice board advertising Keynes Country Park, turn left over a stile in a hedge ❺ and turn right onto a path between a hedge bordering the road on the right and the tree-fringed lake shore on the left. Now comes a most attractive finale to the walk as you follow the path to the left to continue along the lake shore. On emerging into meadowland at the end of the lake, turn left again to return to the start. ●

*Somerford Keynes church*

# Milton under Wychwood and Fifield

| | |
|---|---|
| **Start** | Milton under Wychwood |
| **Distance** | 6 miles (9.7km) |
| **Approximate time** | 3 hours |
| **Parking** | Roadside parking at Milton under Wychwood |
| **Refreshments** | Pub at Milton under Wychwood |
| **Ordnance Survey maps** | Landranger 163 (Cheltenham & Cirencester), Explorer OL45 (The Cotswolds) |

*Much of the first part of this walk on the western side of the Evenlode Valley is through the beautiful woodlands surrounding Bruern Abbey, parts of which form the Foxholes Nature Reserve. After emerging from the woods, the rest of the route is across more open country, heading up to the small village of Fifield before returning across fields to the start.*

The suffix 'under Wychwood' indicates that Milton, along with the neighbouring villages of Shipton and Ascott, was situated beneath the wooded slopes of the medieval royal hunting forest of Wychwood.

🥾 Begin at the road junction by the Quart Pot pub and go through a metal gate into a recreation ground. Head straight across the grass and on the far side, just beyond a tennis court, go through a metal kissing-gate and turn left. Continue along the left-hand edge of three fields and, in the corner of the third one, in front of a cottage, turn left through another metal kissing-gate.

Walk along an enclosed path, cross a footbridge over a brook, keep ahead along a tree-lined path and climb a stile onto a lane. Turn right and after ½ mile (800m), turn left **A** through a gate, at an Oxfordshire Way sign, and walk along an enclosed path. To the right are pleasant views across the Evenlode

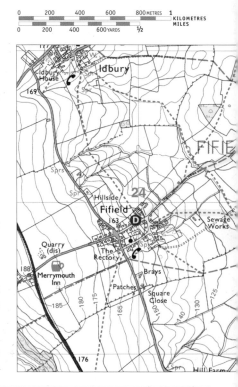

Valley. Go through a gate, continue along the left-hand field edge and in the corner follow the path into trees. Bear slightly right, and now comes a particularly attractive part of the route as you continue along a broad green ride with a fine view in front of Bruern Abbey, a handsome 18th-century mansion built near the site of a vanished medieval abbey.

At the end of the ride, go through a hedge gap, keep ahead across a field, go through a gate and continue along the left-hand field edge. Where the fence turns left, keep ahead to a bridleway sign and then bear slightly left to follow

a path across an avenue of trees – Bruern Abbey is to the right – to go through a gate. Cross a road, go through the gate opposite, keep by the right-hand edge of trees and go through another gate to enter the woodland, part of the Foxholes Nature Reserve.

Continue through this delightful woodland, briefly beside the River Evenlode on the right, to a bridleway sign and turn left up to a track **B**. Turn left along it, go through a gate, keep along the left-hand edge of a field and at its far, tapering end, go through another gate. Continue through more beautiful woodland – keeping in a

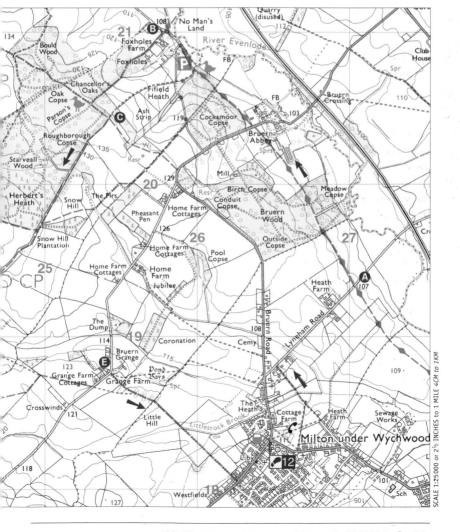

straight line and ignoring all side turns – and at a waymarked post in front of a nature reserve notice, turn left. Just before emerging from the trees into a field, turn right **C** to walk first along the left, inside edge of the wood and then continue in a straight line along a track through the wood.

Where the track bends right at the corner of the wood, keep ahead through a gate, continue gently downhill along an enclosed path, cross a brook and go through a hedge gap. Now head uphill to go through a gate and continue uphill along a track into the small village of Fifield **D**. Turn left along the lane, bearing right if you wish to see the medieval church, noted for its 14th-century octagonal tower topped by a short spire. Otherwise turn left again along a track by cottages, go through a gate and head downhill across a field. Go through another gate, bear right diagonally downhill across a field, climb a stile and continue downhill across the next field. Go through a metal gate, head across the next field to climb a ladder-stile and turn right across a meadow to a stile on the far side. After climbing it, take the path ahead, which cuts across a field corner and then continues parallel to the left-hand edge to a gate.

Go through the gate, walk diagonally across the next field, aiming for the right-hand side of farm buildings, and go through another gate onto a lane. Turn left and at both bridleway and footpath signs, turn right **E** through a metal gate and walk along a track.

Where the track ends, go through a gate, walk across a field, cross a brook and keep ahead to go through another gate. Take the path ahead across a field and, on the far side, continue along a track to a road. Turn left into Milton under Wychwood to return to the start.  ●

*Bruern Abbey*

# Seven Springs and the Churn Valley

| | |
|---|---|
| **Start** | Seven Springs, large layby opposite the Seven Springs pub |
| **Distance** | 6 miles (9.7km) |
| **Approximate time** | 3 hours |
| **Parking** | Layby at Seven Springs |
| **Refreshments** | Pub at Seven Springs, pub at Cockleford |
| **Ordnance Survey maps** | Landranger 163 (Cheltenham & Cirencester), Explorer 179 (Gloucester, Cheltenham & Stroud) |

*From Seven Springs, the route takes you through the Churn Valley, passing through the small villages of Coberley and Cowley. After crossing the river, it follows tracks along the eastern side of the valley to return to the start. There are medieval churches in both villages, pubs at the start and approximate halfway point, and fine views over a tranquil landscape.*

For long, Seven Springs was considered to be one of the sources of the Thames but it is only the source of the River Churn, one of its many tributaries.

🖉 Facing the pub, turn right along the main road and, at a public footpath sign, turn left through a metal kissing-gate **Ⓐ**. Walk along the left-hand edge of three fields, climbing several stiles, and later continue gently downhill along an enclosed path into Coberley.

Keep ahead along a lane, turn left to continue through the village to a T-junction and turn left. Just beyond the sign to Coberley Church, turn right **Ⓑ** through a gate by a cottage and walk along the right-hand edge of a field to a gate. Go through and keep along the left-hand edge of the next field. There is an attractive view of the church to the right, which was mainly rebuilt in the 19th century but retains its medieval tower and south chapel.

After going through a metal gate, continue across the end of a pool to go through another metal gate, veer slightly left across the next field and go through a gate onto an enclosed tarmac track.

Turn right gently downhill, turn first left and then right around the side of a house to cross the infant River Churn, continue along a tree-lined path but almost immediately turn left over a stile, at a public footpath sign **Ⓒ**. Walk along the left-hand field edge, bear left across the field corner into a belt of trees and cross a footbridge. Ascend steps, turn right by a wire fence on the left but almost immediately bear right along a faint path through young conifers to a waymarked post. Turn left to a gate, go through and walk along the right-hand field edge, looking out for a waymarked stile on the right.

Climb the stile, bear left across a field

| 0 | 200 | 400 | 600 | 800 METRES | 1 |
| | | | | | KILOMETRES MILES |
| 0 | 200 | 400 | 600 YARDS | ½ | |

– passing along the left-hand edge of a circle of trees – climb a stile and continue across the next field, keeping by a wall on the right, to climb another stile. Continue along a track to a lane and keep ahead into the estate village of Cowley. Here there is the classic English combination of great house and church side by side. The former – now a nursing home – is a huge 19th-century mansion and the latter – an attractive medieval church – was heavily restored when the house was built.

In the village, follow the lane around a right-hand bend and take the first turning on the left **D**, signposted to Gloucestershire Guide Headquarters. The lane soon bends left and you keep along it for nearly ½ mile (800m) to a T-junction in front of the Green Dragon Inn at Cockleford. Turn right, take the first lane on the left **E** – signposted 'Cockleford, No Through Road' – and where it bends right in front of a house, turn left through trees and walk along an enclosed path, which descends to cross a footbridge over the River Churn. Keep ahead along a tarmac drive that winds uphill to a road **F**.

Take the uphill tarmac track opposite. After passing houses, it continues as a broad, rough track climbing gently between fields, with fine views to the left over the Churn Valley. The track eventually descends to a lane. Turn right, passing by farms, and at a T-junction turn left **G**. Ignore the first Cotswold Way sign, continue along the lane for another ¼ mile (400km) but at the second one – where the lane bends left – keep ahead along a track **H**. This track later descends to a gate. Go through onto the main road at Seven Springs by a junction and keep ahead along the A436 to the start. ●

_The Churn Valley_

# Adlestrop, Evenlode and Chastleton

| | |
|---|---|
| **Start** | Adlestrop |
| **Distance** | 6 miles (9.7km) |
| **Approximate time** | 3 hours |
| **Parking** | Adlestrop, village hall car park |
| **Refreshments** | None |
| **Ordnance Survey maps** | Landranger 163 (Cheltenham & Cirencester), Explorer OL45 (The Cotswolds) |

*The walk is in the gentle countryside of the Evenlode Valley and there are a series of fine views across the valley. Three quiet and highly attractive villages – all with interesting medieval churches – are passed through and there is an opportunity to visit a fine 17th-century house.*

YES, I remember Adlestrop –
*The name, because one afternoon
Of heat the express-train drew up
    there
Unwontedly. It was late June.*

*The steam hiss'd. Some one clear'd
    his throat.
No one left and no one came
On the bare platform. What I saw
Was Adlestrop – only the name ...*

Edward Thomas's poem, written just before the First World War, has immortalised the name of this tiny Cotswold village, as well as vividly evoking the heyday of rural rail travel, when even small and remote villages like this were linked to the outside world without losing their tranquillity or sense of remoteness. Adlestrop could hardly be more perfect: golden stone cottages, many of them thatched, situated close to the great house, which dates mainly from the 16th to the 18th century, and

the whole of this gentle and old-fashioned scene presided over by a medieval church.

🖊 Turn left out of the car park and immediately turn left again along a track. To the right is a small shelter which houses the old station nameplate – placed here, after the station was closed in the 1960s, as a tribute to Edward Thomas, one of the war poets, killed in action in 1917. After climbing a stile, keep ahead across a field, joining a hedge on the left, and climb a stile in the corner. Walk along a left-hand field edge, climb another stile at a way-marked post and continue along the right-hand edge of the next field. Climb a stile and head gently uphill across a field to a stile on the far side. After climbing it, head uphill through a belt of trees, continue across a field and go through a metal gate in the far right corner **Ⓐ**.

Turn left, immediately go through a gate and walk along a gently descending,

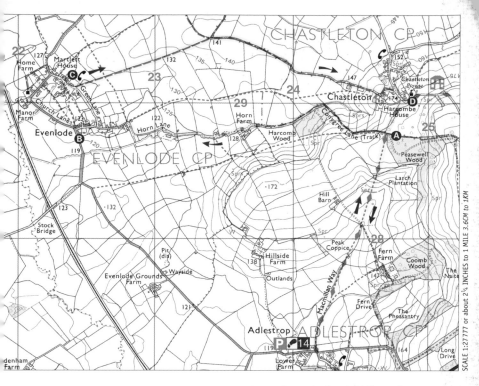

SCALE 1:27777 or about 2¼ INCHES to 1 MILE 3.6CM to 1KM

```
0      200    400    600    800 METRES  1
                                        KILOMETRES
                                        MILES
0      200    400    600 YARDS  ½
```

enclosed path called Conygree Lane.
The route continues along the left-hand
edge of fields, eventually emerging
onto a tarmac drive. Follow this winding drive – which later becomes a lane
(Horn Lane) – into the quiet and remote
village of Evenlode. Turn left at a
T-junction **B**, follow the lane around a
right-hand bend, passing the medieval
church, and turn right at the next
T-junction.

Pass to the left of a green and at the
end of it turn left over a stile, at a public
bridleway sign **C**. Walk along the left-
hand edge of a series of fields and, in
the corner of the fourth and final one,
turn left through a gate. Turn right to
continue along an attractive, tree-lined
track, which eventually ascends to a
T-junction. Turn left along a tarmac
track that bends right to a lane and
turn right.

Just before the lane bends left, the
route continues to the right through a
gate **D** but just beyond the bend is
Chastleton House and church. The
house, a fine, unspoilt Jacobean
mansion, now owned by the National
Trust, was built by a local wool
merchant in the early 17th century
after purchasing the estate from Robert
Catesby, a co-conspirator in the
Gunpowder Plot. Inside it has fine
panelling and furniture, and its most
outstanding features are the Great Hall
and the Long Gallery on the top floor,
which has a magnificent ceiling. The
combination of great house, small
village and simple church, which
dates back to Norman times, in close
proximity could not be more attractive
or traditional.

After going through the gate, walk
along a track, go through another gate
and continue along a tree-lined track.
To the right are fine views over the wide
Evenlode Valley. On reaching a metal
gate **A**, you rejoin the outward route
and retrace your steps to the start. ●

# *Sharpness and Berkeley*

| | |
|---|---|
| **Start** | Sharpness, picnic site near dock, signposted at end of B4066 |
| **Distance** | 6½ miles (10.5km) |
| **Approximate time** | 3 hours |
| **Parking** | Picnic site at Sharpness |
| **Refreshments** | Pub at Sharpness, pubs at Berkeley |
| **Ordnance Survey maps** | Landranger 162 (Gloucester & Forest of Dean), Explorer 167 (Thornbury, Dursley & Yate) |

*This walk in the flat countryside adjoining the Severn Estuary begins by following an old track from Sharpness into Berkeley, famed for its medieval castle. It returns to the estuary alongside the meandering Berkeley Pill, and the last mile (1.6km) of the route is beside the river. In such flat terrain the views are extensive, ranging from the Cotswold escarpment in the east to the wooded slopes of the Forest of Dean in the west across the estuary.*

The small port of Sharpness grew up where the Gloucester and Sharpness Canal, opened in 1827, empties into the Severn Estuary.

📷 Start by turning right out of the car park along Great Western Road, passing a row of cottages, turn left at a T-junction and, at a crossroads, turn right. Bear left along a tarmac path, at a Severn Way sign, go through a metal kissing-gate and keep ahead across a field.

Go through two more kissing-gates in quick succession, cross a railway line and continue along a tarmac path to a road Ⓐ. There is a pub just to the left. Turn right, at a junction keep ahead along Sanigar Lane and pass under a railway bridge to a T-junction. Turn left, in the Berkeley direction, and after almost ½ mile (800m), turn right onto a tarmac track Ⓑ. The track curves left and continues as a broad, rough, hedge-

lined track for the next mile (1.6km), eventually heading uphill to emerge onto a road on the edge of Berkeley Ⓒ.

Turn right and follow the road into the Market Place in the centre of the small town. Turn left, almost immediately turn right along High Street and turn left up Church Street to visit Berkeley's three main attractions: Jenner Museum, church and castle. First comes the museum to Dr Edward Jenner (1749–1823), the pioneer of smallpox vaccination. Beyond that is the 13th-century church, with its fine array of lancet windows on the west front. Jenner is buried in the church and there are many tombs and monuments to the Berkeley family.

To gain access to Berkeley Castle, turn left on entering the churchyard – passing by the detached 18th-century bell tower – and just before going under a bridge, turn right up steps to the castle

entrance. This grand 12th-century fortress has been the ancestral home of the Berkeleys since the Middle Ages and is perhaps best known for the horrific death of Edward II, murdered here in 1327 on the orders of his wife. The dungeon where this took place can still be seen. The buildings are grouped around the great Norman keep, and

*The Severn Estuary at Sharpness*

since the castle was largely remodelled in the 14th century, its external appearance has remained largely unchanged. Inside it has been transformed from a bleak medieval castle into a stately home and contains a fine collection of paintings, furniture, tapestries, silver and porcelain. The attractive grounds include an Elizabethan terraced garden.

Return to High Street and turn left *(at this point a brief detour ahead, turning left at a public footpath sign to Woodford into a meadow rewards you with a fine view of the castle)*. Otherwise, the route continues to the right along Jumpers Lane **D**. Where the lane turns right, keep ahead beside a metal gate and walk across grass in front of

cottages to climb a stile. Now you keep above Berkeley Pill, following the meanderings of the stream over footbridges and a series of stiles to finally climb a metal stile onto a road to the right of a bridge **E**.

Cross over, climb a stile opposite – here joining the Severn Way – and continue above the winding pill, climbing more stiles. Eventually the path takes you to the top of a broad embankment and, after going through a metal gate, you reach the Severn estuary. The path curves right to keep alongside the river back to the start. Approaching Sharpness, climb a metal stile, turn right along the edge of a grassy area, passing by the end of a row of cottages, and continue along a road. Turn left to return to the picnic site. ●

# Deerhurst, Apperley and the River Severn

| | |
|---|---|
| **Start** | Deerhurst, by Odda's Chapel, signposted from B4213 |
| **Distance** | 7 miles (11.3km) |
| **Approximate time** | 3½ hours |
| **Parking** | Deerhurst |
| **Refreshments** | Pub near Mumford's Farm, pub at Haw Bridge, pub on riverside path |
| **Ordnance Survey maps** | Landrangers 150 (Worcester & The Malverns) and 162 (Gloucester & Forest of Dean), Explorer 179 (Gloucester, Cheltenham & Stroud) |

*From Deerhurst, noted for its Saxon church and chapel, the route crosses fields to Apperley and continues by the banks of a disused canal to reach the River Severn. The final three miles (4.8km) is a pleasant and relaxing walk beside the river, following the Severn Way. As this is an almost entirely flat walk, there are wide and extensive views in all directions, eastwards to the line of the Cotswolds and westwards – across the river – to the impressive profile of the Malverns.*

Saxon churches are something of a rarity but in the small village of Deerhurst there are two. The walk starts by Odda's Chapel, a small late-Saxon chapel built by Odda, a kinsman of Edward the Confessor, in 1056. Nearby is the church which, although mainly medieval, retains some of its original Saxon stonework, arches and doorways. It was founded as a monastery, probably during the 8th century, and was a place of some importance in Saxon England but declined after the Norman Conquest with the rise of the great abbeys of Evesham, Tewkesbury and Gloucester in the locality. After its suppression in the 15th century, it became a parish church.

🖉 Where the lane ends at the car park, turn left over a stile, at a public footpath sign, and walk diagonally across a field in the direction indicated by a yellow arrow. Look out for a stile on the right at the end of a line of trees and head across to climb it. Continue across the next field and climb a stile in the far corner onto a narrow lane.

Turn right, follow the lane around a left-hand bend and at a right-hand bend, keep ahead **Ⓐ**, passing to the left of a gate, to a stile. Climb it, walk along an enclosed path, by a young plantation on the right, climb another stile and keep straight ahead across a field to climb a stile on the far side. Keep in the same direction across a playing field to a road, turn right and, at a public footpath sign, turn left over a stile. Continue by a fence on the left, climb a stile in the field corner, keep ahead to

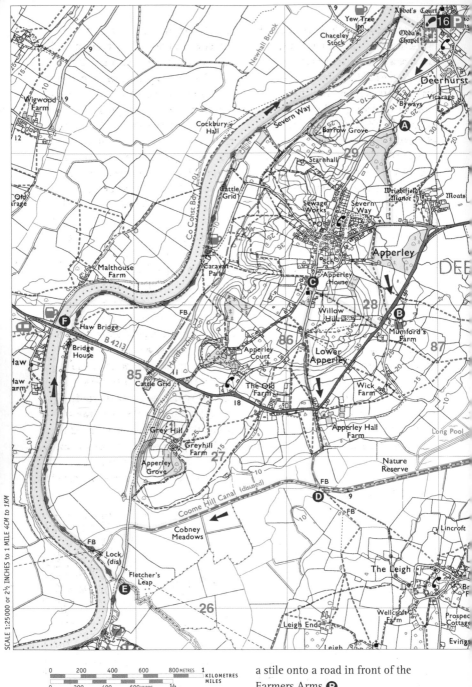

| 0 | 200 | 400 | 600 | 800 METRES | 1 |
| 0 | 200 | 400 | 600 YARDS | ½ | |

KILOMETRES
MILES

climb another, walk across the end of a garden and climb another stile. Bear slightly left across a field, climb a stile in the far corner, continue in the same direction across the next field and climb

a stile onto a road in front of the Farmers Arms **Ⓑ**.

Turn right and, at a public footpath sign, turn right over a stile and head gently uphill in a straight line between widely spaced trees. In the top, right-hand corner, climb two stiles in quick succession and continue over the brow of a hill to another stile. Climb it, walk across the next field, climb a stile, continue across the next field and climb a stile in the right-hand corner. Walk along a fence-lined path to emerge onto a lane in Apperley ❸. The main part of the village – with its green, pond and brick-built church – is to the right.

Turn left and at a public bridleway sign – where the lane bears right in front of a new housing estate – turn left onto an enclosed path. This attractive, tree-lined path descends gently to a road. Cross over and continue along the enclosed track opposite. The track later bends right, turns left in front of a gate and finally crosses a footbridge to a T-junction ❶. Turn right along a path that keeps beside the disused Coome Hill Canal on the left for just over ¾ mile (1.2km), eventually going through a gate onto a lane. The canal was built in 1796 to link the coalfields of the Forest of Dean with Cheltenham. It closed in 1876, and the area is now a nature reserve.

Turn left along the lane to cross a bridge over the disused canal and after ¼ mile (400km) turn right over a stile to join the Severn Way ❸. Walk across a meadow, bearing right to keep parallel with the riverbank, and at its far edge turn first right and then left to climb a stile. Bear left across the next meadow and climb two stiles in quick succession. Now continue along the riverbank to a road, climbing several stiles. In the last field before the road, look out for a stile on the left about half-way along it. Climb the stile, turn right and head across to climb another one and walk along a track, passing to the left of a house. At a fork, take the left-hand path, which heads up to the road to the right of Haw Bridge ❻.

Cross over, climb the stile opposite and continue by the River Severn back to Deerhurst. At one point the route keeps along the edge of a caravan site and passes the Coalhouse Inn but otherwise it is mainly across meadows beside the river, crossing several stiles. Soon after passing the Yew Tree Inn on the opposite side of the river, you see Odda's Chapel over to the right. At a public footpath sign in front of a large, solitary oak tree, turn right along a track and go through a gate to return to the start. ●

*The Saxon church at Deerhurst*

# Lechlade, Kelmscott and the River Thames

| | |
|---|---|
| **Start** | Lechlade |
| **Distance** | 7½ miles (12.1km) |
| **Approximate time** | 3½ hours |
| **Parking** | Lechlade |
| **Refreshments** | Pubs and cafés at Lechlade, pub at St John's Bridge, pub at Kelmscott |
| **Ordnance Survey maps** | Landranger 163 (Cheltenham & Cirencester), Explorer 170 (Abingdon, Wantage & Vale of White Horse) |

*This is an entirely flat walk, which begins by heading across meadows and along lanes into the village of Kelmscott, with its manor house and tiny church. Here you join the Thames Path, and the remainder of the route is along the banks of the meandering river. The final stretch across riverside meadows, between St John's Bridge and Ha'penny Bridge, is especially memorable, with fine views of the tower and spire of Lechlade church.*

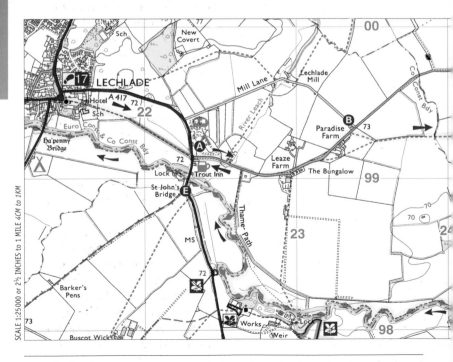

Lechlade lies on the north bank of the River Thames in the south-east corner of Gloucestershire, near the borders with Oxfordshire and Wiltshire. It is an attractive little town, clustered around its handsome Market Place and dominated by an imposing 15th-century church. The latter, one of the great 'wool churches' of the Cotswolds, has a tower and slender spire visible for miles around across the flat terrain of the upper Thames valley. Inside it is light and spacious with a superb chancel roof. The churchyard inspired some of Shelley's verses, and the opening part of the route is called 'Shelley's Walk'.

The walk begins in the Market Place by the church. Take the paved path to the left of the church, cross a lane, go through a metal kissing-gate and walk along a straight tarmac path. Go through a kissing-gate, keep ahead to go through another one and continue along an attractive, tree-lined path, which emerges

onto a road to the left of St John's Bridge **A**. Take the lane opposite and after ¾ mile (1.2km) turn right over a stile **B** at a public footpath sign, and walk diagonally across a field. Climb a stile in the corner, keep along the left-hand edge of the next two fields and, at a hedge corner, continue across the field to cross a footbridge over a brook on the far side. Head straight across the next field towards the far right corner, where you emerge onto a lane at a bend.

Keep ahead to Kelmscott church, a small but interesting building of Norman origin, virtually unaltered since the 16th century. Inside are some medieval wall paintings. The grave of William Morris, 19th-century poet, craftsman and social reformer, who lived at the nearby manor, is in the churchyard. Just beyond the church, turn right along a lane **C** and, after passing the Plough Inn, the lane curves left into the small village. At a T-junction, turn right along a lane which ends by Kelmscott Manor, an Elizabethan house that was the home of William Morris from 1871 until his death in 1896. The house contains many of his possessions, including ceramics, furniture and textiles.

Bear left to continue along a track to the River Thames and turn sharp right, crossing a footbridge and going through a gate, to join the Thames Path **D**. Keep by the river, negotiating several gates and stiles, and look out for where a Thames Path sign directs you to turn left to cross a footbridge over an arm of the river. Climb a stile, follow the river round a right-hand bend and climb another stile to emerge at Buscot Lock. Follow the tarmac path to the right to recross an arm of the river. Do not climb the stile here but continue by the meandering Thames, climbing a succession of stiles. After going through a metal gate, immediately turn left to cross a footbridge over the river, go through another gate and turn right to continue along the left bank of the Thames. Cross a footbridge over a channel, keep ahead and go through a gate to pass under St John's Bridge. **E** Walk past St John's Lock, go through another gate and follow the Thames across lovely riverside meadows to Ha'penny Bridge.

All the way there are fine views looking upstream to the spire of Lechlade church. After passing under the bridge, turn sharp left up steps to the road. Turn left over the bridge, keep ahead into Lechlade and, at a T-junction, turn right back to the Market Place.

*St John's Lock with Lechlade church in the background*

# Stow-on-the-Wold, Broadwell and Donnington

| | |
|---|---|
| **Start** | Stow-on-the-Wold |
| **Distance** | 6 miles (9.7km) |
| **Approximate time** | 3 hours |
| **Parking** | Stow-on-the-Wold |
| **Refreshments** | Pubs and cafés at Stow-on-the-Wold, pub at Broadwell |
| **Ordnance Survey maps** | Landranger 163 (Cheltenham & Cirencester), Explorer OL45 (The Cotswolds) |

*Although there seems to be a high proportion of road-walking on this route, the vast majority of it is along attractive, peaceful and tree-lined lanes. Only the last ¾ mile (1.2km) into Stow-on-the-Wold is along a fairly busy road and this is made acceptable by a wide verge all the way. In between are quiet tracks and field paths, attractive and unspoilt villages and extensive views over rolling wold country, which together make up a highly enjoyable and interesting walk.*

The major route centre of Stow-on-the-Wold lies 755ft (230m) up on the exposed wolds. The focal point of this attractive and popular little town is the large and bustling market square, lined by mainly 17th- and 18th-century buildings and containing a large number of gift and antique shops, inns, restaurants and teashops to cater for the many visitors. In one corner of the square is the medieval church, restored in the 17th century after being damaged while housing Civil War prisoners.

🖉 The walk begins in the middle of the market square in front of St Edward's Hall, now the library. Turn right across to the corner of the square, walk along High Street and turn right into Parson's Corner. At a T-junction,

turn left along a narrow lane, passing some of the town wells, and just after bearing left in front of a house, the lane first becomes an enclosed track and then narrows to a path.

This attractive, tree-lined path emerges onto a lane **Ⓐ**, and you turn right gently downhill into Broadwell. At a T-junction in front of the spacious green, turn left **Ⓑ** in the Donnington and Moreton-in-Marsh direction, pass the Fox Inn and, where the lane bends right, keep ahead, at a public footpath sign, along a path to a gate. Go through, continue across grass – later by a wall on the left – and go through a kissing-gate into Broadwell churchyard. The church dates from the 12th century, was enlarged in the 13th, and the tower was built in the 15th century. In the churchyard at the east end of the church is a fine collection of 'wool bale' tombs, so called because they supposedly represent corded bales of wool.

Passing to the left of the church, go through a gate and turn right to a T-junction. Turn left and follow the lane over the A429 and ahead into the hamlet of Donnington. At a fork in front of a barn, take the left-hand lane, turn right at a T-junction and, where the lane turns right, keep ahead along a track. Turn left through a waymarked metal gate **C** and walk along the left-edge of two fields, climbing a stile. In the corner of the second field, climb a stone stile and turn half-right across the next field to a waymarked post. Turn left to continue along the right-hand field edge, climb a stile, bear left and head downhill across a field to cross a footbridge over a ditch at the bottom.

Bear slightly right across the next, long field, making for a waymarked stile in the corner, and, after climbing it, keep ahead along an enclosed, tree-lined track to emerge onto the A424 **D**.

Take the lane ahead and turn left, in the Upper Swell direction, along a lane that descends, passes by the picturesque Donnington Brewery, crosses the little River Dickler and continues to a road **E**.

Bear left into Upper Swell and, at a Gloucestershire Way and public footpath sign to Lower Swell, turn right

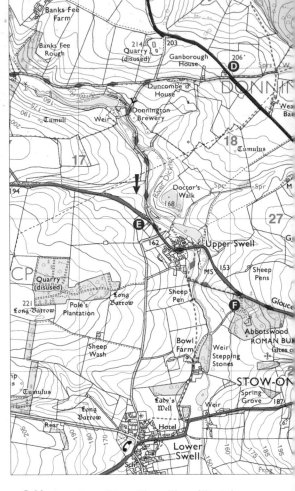

through a metal gate. Immediately go through another and continue across two fields, negotiating two stiles. After the second of these, turn left along a narrow, enclosed path to cross a footbridge over the River Dickler.

Climb a stile, walk gently uphill along the right-hand field edge, climb over a stile in the corner and go through a wrought-iron gate onto the road **F**.

Turn right, following the road back to Stow-on-the-Wold and at a crossroads keep ahead along High Street to return to the market square. ●

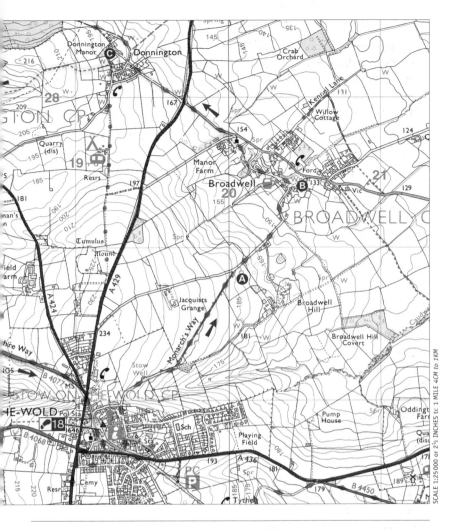

*Donnington Brewery*

*Painswick and the Beacon*

# Painswick and the Beacon

| | |
|---|---|
| **Start** | Painswick |
| **Distance** | 6 miles (9.7km) |
| **Approximate time** | 3 hours |
| **Parking** | Painswick |
| **Refreshments** | Pubs and cafés at Painswick |
| **Ordnance Survey maps** | Landranger 162 (Gloucester & Forest of Dean), Explorer 179 (Gloucester, Cheltenham & Stroud) |

*From the delightful town of Painswick, the route takes you via field paths, tracks and lanes to the summit of Painswick Hill (Beacon), 928ft (283m) high and a magnificent viewpoint. You then join the Cotswold Way for an easy descent, mainly through woodland, back into the town. Although an undulating walk, none of the ascents or descents are steep or strenuous, and the final climb to the Beacon is relatively undemanding.*

In an area of appealing small towns, Painswick must rank among the finest. Occupying a ridge between two valleys, it has a sloping main street, narrow side streets, fine medieval church and a wealth of dignified and attractive houses, all built from creamy-coloured stone. Most of its buildings date from the 17th and 18th centuries, Painswick's heyday as an important centre of the wool trade and cloth-dyeing industry. The church has a 15th-century tower topped by a tall spire, and the churchyard possesses a splendid collection of tombs.

🖊 Turn right out of the car park and walk up the main street, passing the church. Turn left along the B4073, signposted to Gloucester and Upton St Leonards, and where the road curves right, bear left along a lane. Ⓐ At a T-junction, turn right and almost immediately turn left, at a public footpath sign, along a path through trees. Turn left again along a track, go through a gate and turn right. From here there are pleasant views ahead

across the valley, and the 18th-century façade of Painswick House can be seen to the right. The Rococo Garden adjoining this house has been almost fully restored and is open to the public.

Head downhill along the right-hand edge of two fields, climbing two stiles, and continue along a fence-lined path, by woodland on the right. The route continues along the right-hand edge of a field, heading first up and then down, to reach a stile in the field corner. After climbing it, continue gently uphill again along the right-hand edge of the next field and, just over the crest, go through a metal gate onto a tarmac track. Turn right uphill to a T-junction and turn left along a narrow lane Ⓑ.

The lane descends, bends sharply right in front of Holcombe Farm and continues downhill through woodland, passing the handsome Holcombe House. It then heads uphill and, where the lane curves left at the next farmhouse, bear right Ⓒ at a public footpath sign, onto a track and climb a stile. Head diagonally uphill across a rough field, climb a stile in the far corner and keep ahead towards trees. Climb a stile, walk along a tree-lined path and, on emerging into a field, continue across it – later by a hedge on the right. Painswick Beacon can be seen to the right.

At a fork, take the right-hand path towards a farm, keep ahead along a farm track, passing in front of the buildings, and continue uphill to a lane. Do not turn right along it but take the parallel, yellow-waymarked straight path, which continues through trees to the A46. Turn right and at a public footpath sign bear left along a track **D**. At a fork, take the right-hand track towards the Beacon but after about 20 yds (18m) turn right off it onto a narrow path that continues uphill, by the right edge of woodland. When you see the triangulation pillar on the summit, turn sharp right and head up to it **E**. Painswick Beacon is an area of common land comprising a mixture of open grassland, woodland and disused quarries, and part of it is a golf course. The views from Painswick Hill are magnificent.

Continue along the ridge, bearing right and descending to a path. Turn right and follow it steadily downhill, along the left-hand edge of trees and above a former quarry, to join a broad path. Bear right onto it – the remainder of the walk is along the well-waymarked Cotswold Way – to a lane, turn left and, where the lane bends sharply to the left, turn right along a tarmac track **F**. Pass beside a vehicle barrier to a former quarry, now a craft centre, and in front of the quarry gates take the wooded

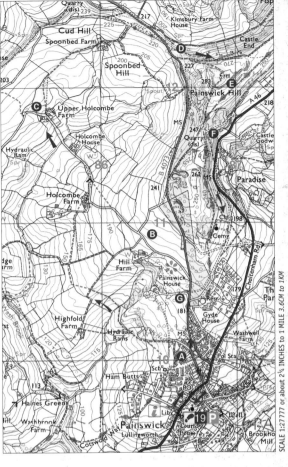

track to the left. At a fork, take the left-hand path to continue through woodland and, on emerging from the trees, bear right across grass to pick up a path that keeps along the right-hand edge of more woodland.

Bear left on joining a track, continue across part of the golf course, cross a tarmac drive and keep ahead across the course into rough grass on the far side. Follow a path first through the grass and then through trees to a lane and turn right. At a T-junction, turn left **G** into Painswick, take the right-hand road at a fork and, where it curves left, pick up the outward route **A** to return to the start.

# Crickley Hill and Leckhampton Hill

| | |
|---|---|
| **Start** | Crickley Hill Country Park |
| **Distance** | 7 miles (11.3km) |
| **Approximate time** | 3½ hours |
| **Parking** | Crickley Hill Country Park |
| **Refreshments** | Pub near end of the walk |
| **Ordnance Survey maps** | Landranger 163 (Cheltenham & Cirencester), Explorer 179 (Gloucester, Cheltenham & Stroud) |

*Two of the finest vantage points on the Cotswold escarpment, both over 870ft (265m) high, are linked by this walk. There is a varied mixture of wooded and more open terrain, and the views from the two hills, over Cheltenham below and across the Vale of Severn to the line of the Malverns, are magnificent, especially in clear conditions. There is plenty of climbing but all the ascents and descents are easy and gradual.*

Crickley Hill Country Park, established in 1979 and comprising a mixture of limestone grassland and woodland, occupies a spur of the Cotswold escarpment. There are superb views, looking across the Vale of Severn to the Malverns on the horizon.

🔎 The first part of the walk is along the Cotswold Way and it starts at the visitor centre. With your back to it, cross a tarmac drive, pass through the car park, go up steps and turn left through a kissing-gate, at a National Trust sign to Crickley Hill. Walk along the ridge and follow a clear, broad path as it bears right to continue through woodland. Climb a stile, continue along the wooded ridge, by a wire fence on the right, and climb two more stiles to descend to a narrow lane **Ⓐ**.

Turn right to a crossroads, keep ahead and, where the lane bears right, turn left along an enclosed path **Ⓑ**, at a public footpath sign to Leckhampton Hill. The path later ascends, continues through trees and finally keeps along a left-hand field edge to a lane **Ⓒ**. Turn left downhill and, at a Cotswold Way sign, turn right onto an enclosed path **Ⓓ**, which heads uphill, initially above a disused quarry. Continue uphill across the open grassland of Leckhampton Hill and, at a sign to the Devil's Chimney, make a brief detour to the left to see it. This limestone pinnacle is not a natural phenomenon but was created by 19th-century quarrymen. Much of Cheltenham, seen below, was built from stone quarried here.

Return to the path, turn left and continue over the hill, passing the view-indicator – another outstanding view-point – and curving right to pass to the left of the triangulation pillar on the summit, a height of 961ft (293m). Keep across the undulating hilltop as far as a

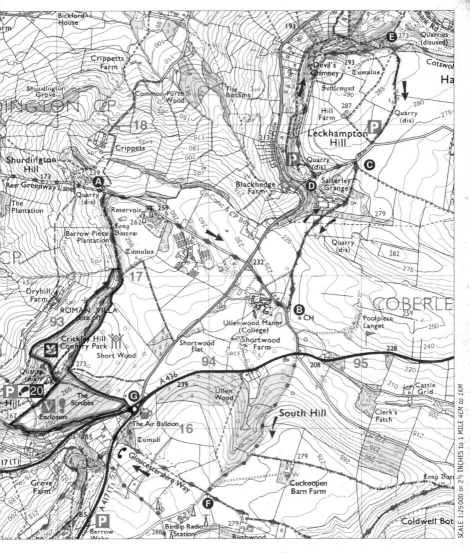

SCALE 1:25 000 or 2½ INCHES to 1 MILE 4CM to 1KM

gate on the right **E**, go through it and walk along an enclosed path, which bears right to reach a pair of gates, one wooden and one metal. Go through either, continue along a straight path through trees to a track and turn left to a lane.

Turn right and, where the lane bears slightly right, turn left onto a path, at a Cotswold Way sign **C**. Here you rejoin the outward route and retrace your steps downhill to where the path emerges onto a lane **B**. Turn left to leave the outward route and follow the lane to the A436. After crossing it, do not take the lane opposite but bear right along a track that heads steadily uphill and later becomes a tarmac track.

After ³/₄ mile (1.2km) you reach a metal gate where a track joins from the left. Do not go through it but turn right, at public footpath and Gloucestershire Way signs **F**, to pass beside another metal gate and walk along the left-hand field edge. Bear left through a hedge gap in the corner, bear right and continue across the next two fields. At the end of the second one, go through a gate and bear right into woodland. Climb a stile and bear left down to the busy A417. Turn right beside the Air Balloon pub, at a traffic island turn left **G** – there are Cotswold Way and public bridleway signs here – and walk down a track to a gate by a National Trust sign 'The Scrubbs'.

Go through it and, at a three-way fork ahead, take the middle path across grass into woodland. Continue steadily uphill – following the regular blue-waymarked posts – go through a gate at the top and turn left along the drive to the visitor centre. ●

*The Devil's Chimney, above Cheltenham*

# Brockhampton, Sevenhampton and Whittington

| | |
|---|---|
| **Start** | Large layby on A40 about 2½ miles (4km) east of Cheltenham and ¼ mile (400km) to west of a side turn to Whittington |
| **Distance** | 6½ miles (10.5km) |
| **Approximate time** | 3½ hours |
| **Parking** | Layby on A40 |
| **Refreshments** | Pub at Brockhampton |
| **Ordnance Survey maps** | Landranger 163 (Cheltenham & Cirencester), Explorer OL45 (The Cotswolds) |

*This walk in the upper Coln Valley links three small, quiet and secluded villages, two of which have interesting and attractive medieval churches and the third a welcoming pub. In between you walk through a typical Cotswold landscape of rolling hills interspersed with stretches of woodland, with a succession of fine views. Expect some of the paths to be muddy and overgrown in places.*

Just beyond the east end of the layby, a public footpath sign directs you to turn left through trees to a stile. Climb it, bear left across a field to climb another stile and continue across the next field, veering left to climb another stile in the corner.

Head diagonally across the next field and on the far side aim for the left-hand edge of a cottage and go through a kissing-gate onto a lane on the edge of Whittington. Turn right and take the first lane on the left **Ⓐ**, which later becomes a tarmac track. At the end of the track, go through a gate and continue gently uphill through woodland, going through two more gates. After the second one, you emerge from the wood and keep ahead across grassland – there

is a disused quarry on the right – later continuing by a hedge on the left to a metal gate. Go through, keep ahead and at a fork take the right-hand path (blue waymark here), which bears slightly right and keeps by a hedge on the left. The path later becomes tree-lined and continues to a gate.

Go through, walk along the left-hand edge of woodland to a T-junction, turn right to head steadily uphill through the trees, go through a metal gate and continue uphill along the right-hand edge of a field. At a crossing of paths – by a stile on the right – keep ahead alongside a wire fence and turn left in the field corner to continue along its right-hand edge. After passing through a wide gap into the next field, head

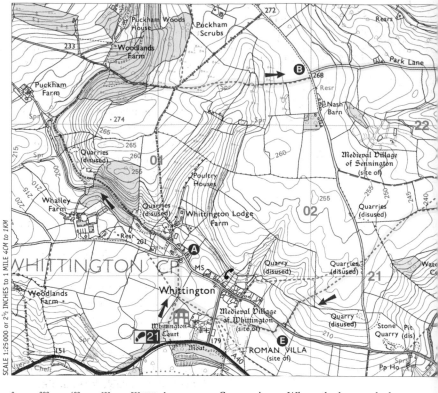

SCALE 1:25000 or 2½ INCHES to 1 MILE 4CM to 1KM

| 0 | 200 | 400 | 600 | 800 METRES | 1 |
|---|---|---|---|---|---|
| | | | | | KILOMETRES |
| | | | | | MILES |
| 0 | 200 | 400 | 600 YARDS | ½ | |

gently downhill, passing two way-marked posts and continuing down to climb a stile.

Bear slightly left to climb another stile and keep ahead uphill through trees and scrubs to yet another stile. Climb that one, walk along the left-hand field edge, continue uphill through rough grass and finally keep along the left-hand edge of the next two fields, climbing a stile, to finally emerge onto a narrow lane. Turn left, almost immediately turn right **B** in the Winchcombe and Brockhampton direction, and head downhill to a cross-roads by the entrance to Brockhampton Park, a large 19th-century mansion.

Keep ahead, and the lane continues uphill into the village of Brockhampton. About 100 yds (91m) before reaching a road junction and small green, turn right **C** along a lane, passing the

Craven Arms. Where the lane ends, keep ahead along a narrow path, at a public footpath sign 'Sevenhampton via St Andrews Church', which heads down to a metal gate. Go through to cross the infant River Coln, turn left and walk across a field towards farm buildings. Go through a kissing-gate on the far side, keep by a wall on the right and go through another kissing-gate into the churchyard. Turn first right and then left to pass to the left of Seven-hampton's delightful church, a narrow cruciform building that dates back to the Norman period and has a Perpendicular tower.

Go through a gate onto a lane, go through the kissing-gate opposite, at a public footpath sign to Lower Seven-hampton, and follow a path across a field, bearing slightly left to go through a kissing-gate in the corner. Head downhill to cross a footbridge over the River Coln and keep beside the river to a lane **D**. Turn right to cross a footbridge

head across the field to a ladder-stile. Climb it and keep in the same direction across the next field to a lane. Bear left to enter a field and at a fork take the left-hand path across the field and climb a stone stile on the far side. Head downhill in the same direction across the next field, climb another stile and continue first through a belt of trees and then along a right field edge. Turn right over a stile and bear left to climb another stile onto a lane **E**.

Cross over, walk along the right-hand edge of a field and follow the field edge to the right to a stile. Climb it, bear slightly left across the next field, making for a kissing-gate on the far side, and go through it onto a lane opposite Whittington Court, a grand 16th-century mansion. Next to it is the tiny Norman church, which has a bellcote instead of a tower. The interior is particularly notable for some fine 14th-century effigies.

Go through a kissing-gate to the right of the entrance to the house and keep ahead to a stile. Climb it, continue by the left-hand field edge, climb a stile in the corner and immediately turn left over another one. Here you rejoin the outward route and retrace your steps to the start. ●

beside a ford, head uphill beneath a canopy of trees to a T-junction and keep ahead through trees, at a public footpath sign, to a stile.

Climb it, continue uphill along the right-hand field edge, climb a stone stile and keep along the right-hand edge of the next field as far as a footpath post, where you bear left and

*Sevenhampton church*

# Avon Valley

| | |
|---|---|
| **Start** | Saltford |
| **Distance** | 7 miles (11.3km) |
| **Approximate time** | 3½ hours |
| **Parking** | Saltford Picnic Site |
| **Refreshments** | Pub at Saltford, pub at Swineford, pub at Kelston |
| **Ordnance Survey maps** | Landranger 172 (Bristol & Bath), Explorer 155 (Bristol & Bath) |

*The area of the Avon Valley covered by this walk lies between Bath and Bristol, and there are distant views of both cities from some of the higher points. Particularly outstanding is the view over Bath from Prospect Stile on the Cotswold Way. Both the climb out of the valley to the village of North Stoke and onto the ridge and the descent back to the river are relatively undemanding. Part of the route uses the Bristol and Bath Railway Path, and there is a short stretch of riverside walking.*

Begin by walking along the road, with the River Avon on the right, and at the end of a grassy area, bear right, at a sign 'Permissive Path', along a path between bushes. Ascend steps and turn left along the Bristol and Bath Railway Path, the disused track of the former Midland Railway. The railway closed in the early 1970s but was later converted into a tarmac footpath and cycleway between the two cities.

Just after crossing a bridge over the river, turn left down steps **A** at a T-junction, turn sharp left to pass under the bridge and continue along the right-hand edge of a succession of fields beside the Avon, finally climbing a stile onto a road at Swineford **B**. Take the track opposite, pass through a farmyard and continue along a tarmac track to a picnic site, created on the site of a former iron foundry. At a wall corner – just before reaching the car park – turn right, walk across to climb a stile, head across a field

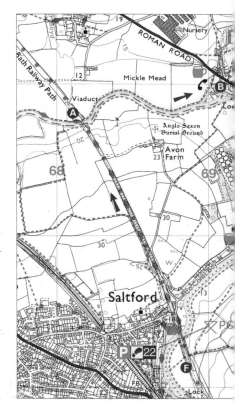

and climb a double stile on the far side. Continue uphill across the next field and pass through a belt of trees to a stile.

After climbing it, turn right along a lovely tree-lined path, which continues uphill, winding round to a T-junction. Turn right along a walled track into North Stoke, turn left along an uphill lane and, where it ends, bear left at a public bridleway sign, along a track **C**. Turn right through a metal gate, pass to the left of the restored medieval church up to a stile, climb it and turn right to keep first alongside the churchyard wall and then along the right-hand edge of a field. At a waymarked post, bear left uphill across the field to climb a stile and continue quite steeply uphill across the next field, making for a waymarked post and continuing past it to a fence corner. Here you join the Cotswold Way and keep by a fence on the left to a metal kissing-gate.

Go through and follow a grassy path across the middle of Little Down prehistoric fort. At the far end, turn right alongside the earthworks of the fort, keep ahead to a field corner and turn left to continue along the right-hand edge of two fields. In the corner of the second field you reach Prospect Stile **D**, a superb viewpoint over Bath and the Avon Valley, with the Mendips on the horizon. A view-indicator enables you to identify all the places that can be seen in clear conditions.

Go through a kissing-gate, turn left downhill along a narrow path through bushes and the path curves right to a T-junction. Turn right, go through a tall kissing-gate and continue downhill. In the field corner, turn right onto an enclosed path and after about 200 yds

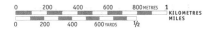

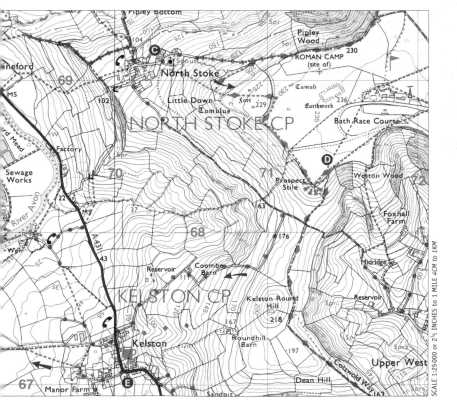

*The River Avon at Saltford*

(183m) look out for a left turn to continue along another enclosed path. The path descends, goes round several bends and turns left at a T-junction by a farm. It later widens into a tarmac track and continues down to a road. Turn left into Kelston and, at a T-junction, turn right **E** along a lane, passing the church over to the left, a medieval building largely rebuilt in 1860.

The lane curves right to a gate, go through and, after a few yards, turn left alongside a fence on the right. Climb a stile, keep ahead and then turn right to climb a stile in the fence and head across to climb another stile. Walk diagonally across a field, in the far corner turn left through a gate and continue along the left-hand edge of the next field. Go through a gate and bear left along a track to a disused railway bridge **F**.

Turn right over a stile in front of the bridge, immediately turn left up steps, turn left again at the top, turn right and right again to briefly rejoin the Bristol and Bath Railway Path. Just after crossing the River Avon, turn left down steps, here rejoining the outward route, and retrace your steps to the start. ●

# Sherborne and Windrush

| | |
|---|---|
| **Start** | Sherborne Park, Ewepen Car Park and Information Centre |
| **Distance** | 7½ miles (12.1km) |
| **Approximate time** | 3½ hours |
| **Parking** | National Trust's Ewepen car park |
| **Refreshments** | None |
| **Ordnance Survey maps** | Landranger 163 (Cheltenham & Cirencester), Explorer OL45 (The Cotswolds) |

*The first and last parts of this most enjoyable and well-waymarked walk are over the well-wooded slopes of Sherborne Park, which occupies a broad ridge above the valley of Sherborne Brook and from which there are fine views across the valley. In between there is much attractive walking across the lush pastures bordering both Sherborne Brook and the River Windrush, and the route passes through the delightful villages of Sherborne and Windrush.*

From the 16th century until 1982, the Sherborne estate was the property of the Dutton family but it is now owned and managed by the National Trust. The Trust has developed an information centre from old farm buildings at Ewepen and has opened up permissive paths across the park, some of which are used on this walk.

Start by turning right out of the car park along a track and, in front of gates, bear left along a grassy path. The first part of the walk follows a dark green-waymarked route. Follow the path around a left-hand bend, later descending through trees, and the path then bends right, crosses a small grassy area, curves right again and continues down through woodland.

At a fork, take the left-hand path, which continues winding downhill to go through a gate onto a road **Ⓐ**. Turn right, passing the entrance to the early 19th-century Sherborne House – now converted into apartments – and church. The latter was mostly rebuilt in the 19th century but retains its medieval tower and spire. Continue on through the attractive estate village to a T-junction. Turn left, at a public footpath sign turn right onto a track **Ⓑ** and continue along an enclosed grassy path to a stile. After climbing it, turn left along a track and, where it bends right, turn left over a stile and walk diagonally across a field, looking out for a waymarked stile to the right of the far corner. Climb it onto a track, turn left, cross a bridge over Sherborne Brook and keep ahead to climb another stile.

Head diagonally across a field, climb a stile, keep ahead first along a track and then along a left-hand field edge, by woodland on the left, and climb two stiles in quick succession. Turn right

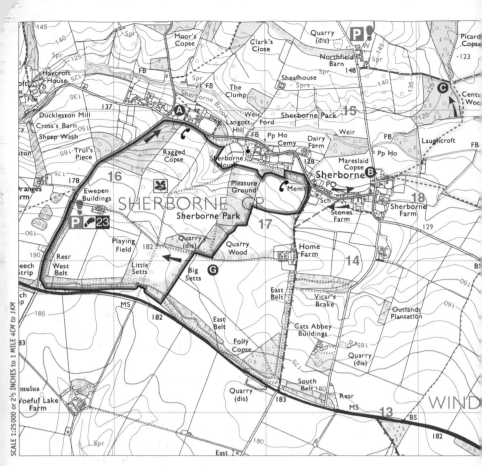

along a track **C** that heads gently downhill by a right-hand field edge, continues as an enclosed track and bears right to a gate. Go through, cross a footbridge over the River Windrush and keep ahead between trees and bushes to emerge into a field.

Turn right **D** onto a broad and undulating track through the valley, following it round first right-hand and then left-hand bends to go through a farmyard, and keep ahead to a metal gate. Do not go through it but turn right along the left-hand field edge, in the corner bear left downhill between trees and bushes, cross a brook and go through a metal gate. Turn left to follow a path across a field, cross a brook, keep in the same direction across the next field and turn right through a metal gate. Keep ahead along a path, curving left to go through a gate, continue curving

*The village of Windrush*

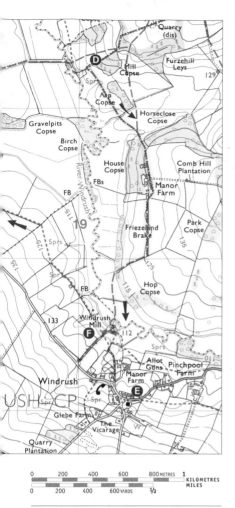

Retrace your steps along the road through the village and keep along it as far as a track beside a cottage. Turn right, passing to the right of the cottage, head gently downhill and, opposite steps on the right leading up to a stone stile, turn left through a gate **F**. Walk across a field – the River Windrush is over to the right – pass between gate-posts and keep along the left-hand edge of the next three fields. At a wall corner in the third field, veer slightly right and continue across the field to a stile on the far side. After climbing it, again keep along the left-hand edge of the next three fields and, just before the corner of the last field, bear right across to a gate. Go through, walk across the next long field, keeping parallel to its right-hand edge, and climb a stile onto a track.

Climb the stone stile opposite, here temporarily rejoining the outward route, and retrace your steps to the post office and war memorial in Sherborne village. Leave the outward route here by going through a gate at the corner of the boundary wall of Sherborne Park – there is a National Trust Sherborne estate sign – and follow a path into trees. For the rest of the walk there are again regular dark green-waymarked posts. The path continues along the left-hand edge of woodland, curves left and heads gently uphill.

Keep ahead at a waymarked post, at the next post turn right into the trees and, on reaching a yew tree with a circular iron seat around it, turn first left, then bear right and continue to a metal gate. After going through, the path bears right, passing to the right of an ice-house, and then bears left to another metal gate. Go through that one, continue through woodland to join a track and bear left along it to a metal gate. Go through, turn right **G** along a track and follow it to the start. ●

left and climb a stile by Windrush Mill. Turn right around the end of the mill building, follow a path to the left and climb a stone stile.

Turn right uphill alongside a wall on the right, climb a stile, keep ahead by a wall on the left and climb another stone stile. Continue along an enclosed path, which first descends and then heads uphill, becomes a tarmac drive and emerges onto a road in the village of Windrush. Turn left to the church **E**, a particularly interesting building with a superb Norman south doorway, beautiful 15th-century nave roof and imposing Perpendicular tower, which overlooks the small, triangular village green.

# Macaroni Downs and the Leach Valley

| Start | Eastleach Turville, by the Victoria Inn |
|---|---|
| Distance | 7½ miles (12.1km) |
| Approximate time | 4 hours |
| Parking | Roadside parking in Eastleach Turville |
| Refreshments | Pub at Eastleach Turville |
| Ordnance Survey maps | Landranger 163 (Cheltenham & Cirencester), Explorer OL45 (The Cotswolds) |

*The opening and closing stretches of the walk are through the lovely Leach Valley, following the elusive and sometimes disappearing small river above the twin villages of Eastleach Turville and Eastleach Martin. In between there is a circuit of the open downland above the valley, returning to the river through woodland. This is a walk in one of the quieter, less-frequented parts of the Cotswolds but has all the classic ingredients of the typical Cotswold landscape: river, woodland, open wold, extensive views and two idyllic villages with fine medieval churches.*

Although only divided by the tiny River Leach, Eastleach Turville and Eastleach Martin are separate small villages, each with its own church, which face each other across the river at a distance of no more than 200 yds (183m).

🖊 Start in front of the Victoria Inn and, facing the pub, turn right along an enclosed tarmac path. At a public footpath sign by a cottage, turn left over a stone stile, walk along an enclosed tarmac path to a lane, turn right and take the first turning on the left. Where the lane ends, go through a metal gate and bear slightly right across a field.

After about 50 yds (46m), bear left and continue across the field to go through a metal gate in the far left corner. Walk along a track, by a wall on

the left, descend gently to go through a metal gate and continue downhill into the valley. Go through another metal gate to the left of a footbridge over the River Leach and keep ahead along the lower slopes of the valley, going through a metal gate and following the curve of the river to eventually emerge onto a lane via another metal gate **Ⓐ**.

Turn right over Sheep Bridge, turn left to go through a gate beside a cattle-grid and immediately turn right and head uphill along the left-hand edge of woodland. Climb a stile at the top, keep ahead but at the corner of the woodland head downhill across the grassy slopes to meet a tarmac track by the edge of woodland **Ⓑ**. Cross it – by a footpath post – and take the track opposite, which ascends gently to a metal gate.

Go through the gate, keep ahead along the right-hand field edge over the Macaroni Downs and go through a metal gate to a crossroads. To the right is a dew pond, thought to date from 1789, and just ahead is a barn. Keep ahead past the barn along the right-hand field edge, go through a gate, continue along the right-hand edge of the next field and bear right to go through another gate. Walk along the left-hand edge of a field, by woodland on the left, and the track bears right to

continue along the left edge. Bear left through a gate to a junction, turn sharp right along a short stretch of hedge-lined track, go through a gate, at a public bridleway sign, and head diagonally across a large field to a waymarked post on the far side.

Continue along the left-hand field edge, pass through a hedge gap to descend to a footpath post, and bear right to go through a gate. Keep in a straight line along the right-hand edge of several fields, later continuing along an enclosed track, which later still becomes a tarmac lane. Continue along the lane and, at a public bridleway sign, turn right **C** onto a path that keeps along the left-hand edge of woodland. At the corner of the wood, keep straight ahead across a field and on the far side go through a gate onto a lane.

Go through the metal gate opposite and walk along the right-hand edge of a field, by woodland on the right again. At a gap in the trees, turn right onto a track and almost immediately turn left to continue along a path through the trees. Keep ahead at a crossing and eventually the path joins and keeps by the little River Leach, a delightful part of the walk.

After exiting from the trees via a metal gate, do not keep ahead beside the river but bear slightly left across the field to a stile. Climb it, keep ahead across a field, veering slightly right to climb a stile in the far right corner, and continue along the edge of the next field by the river again. Turn right over a stile, turn left and continue across riverside meadows, by a wire fence on

*On the Macaroni Downs*

the left, later keeping along a tree-lined path above the meadow to a metal gate. Go through, bear right above the river, passing a stone footbridge, and continue winding across the lower slopes of the valley, finally going through a metal gate onto a lane **D**.

Turn right and follow the lane to a road junction by a small triangular green in front of the medieval church at Eastleach Martin, noted for its Norman doorway and fine 14th-century north transept. The saddleback tower of the mainly 13th-century church at Eastleach Turville on the other side of the river can be seen to the right and involves just a minor detour from the route.

At the junction by the church, keep ahead along the lane signposted to Southrop and Lechlade and, at a public footpath sign, turn right through a gate into the churchyard. Keep to the left of the church, go through another gate, turn left onto a paved path beside the river and turn right to cross a stone footbridge over the river into Eastleach Turville.

This is Keble Bridge, named after the Keble family, who were the local lords of the manor.

Turn left along a lane and follow it as it bears right through the village to return to the starting point. ●

# Cirencester and the Duntisbourne Valley

| | |
|---|---|
| **Start** | Cirencester |
| **Distance** | 8½ miles (13.7km). Shorter version 6 miles (9.7km) |
| **Approximate time** | 4½ hours (3 hours for shorter walk) |
| **Parking** | Cirencester |
| **Refreshments** | Pubs and cafés at Cirencester |
| **Ordnance Survey maps** | Landranger 163 (Cheltenham & Cirencester), Explorers 168 (Stroud, Tetbury & Malmesbury) and 169 (Cirencester & Swindon) |

*From the centre of Cirencester, the walk leads across fields to Stratton and then on through the Duntisbourne Valley to Daglingworth. It continues through the valley to the idyllic hamlet of Duntisbourne Rouse before returning to Daglingworth and taking a different route back to the start. The shorter version omits the extension between Daglingworth and Duntisbourne Rouse. This is a mainly flat walk that encompasses lovely old villages, fine churches and extensive views across rolling country. Leave plenty of time to explore Cirencester, a particularly attractive and interesting old town.*

Cirencester reveals little of its illustrious past as one of the foremost towns of Roman Britain (Corinium) and the seat of a great medieval monastery. Apart from a few feet of wall, plus the remains of an amphitheatre to the south of the town, there is nothing to see of Roman Cirencester, except for the numerous artefacts – including some splendid mosaics – in the excellent Corinium Museum. Also, there is virtually nothing left of the abbey, except for one gateway and the site, which is now an attractive park.

What there is to see is one of the grandest of Cotswold 'wool churches' and some streets of fine old buildings dating from the Middle Ages, when Cirencester developed into one of the

principal centres of the wool trade. The church is magnificent: its spacious interior is almost cathedral-like and the superb Perpendicular tower rises to a height of 162ft (49m). Particularly outstanding is the 15th-century, three-storeyed south porch, which overlooks the Market Place.

The walk starts in the Market Place. Take the paved path that passes in front of the church and continue in a straight line along first Gosditch Street, then Dollar Street, and finally Gloucester Street – passing a series of attractive old buildings – to join the A417. Walk along the main road to where it forks and turn left, at a public footpath sign, onto a track **Ⓐ**. Almost immediately turn right through a

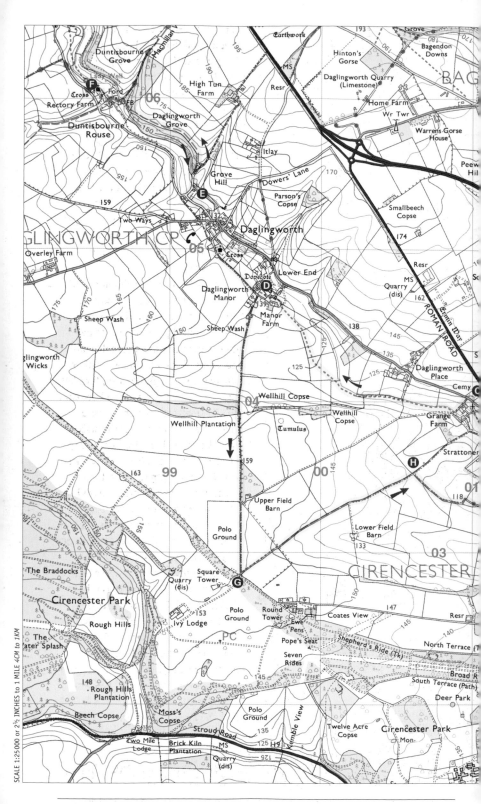

SCALE 1:25000 or 2½ INCHES to 1 MILE 4CM to 1KM

kissing-gate, walk across a field and go through a wall gap on the far side.

Keep ahead along a track, passing in front of houses and bungalows, cross a lane **B** go through a gate opposite and continue along an enclosed path. Go through a gate, walk along a left-hand field edge, go through a metal gate, continue along an enclosed path, cross a tarmac drive and keep ahead to go through another gate onto a track. Go through the kissing-gate opposite, continue initially by a wall on the right and then head across the field to go through another kissing-gate onto a tarmac drive.

Ahead is Stratton's small church, of Norman origin but largely rebuilt in 1850. After entering the churchyard, follow a slabbed path in front of the church, which curves right and heads up to a lane. Turn left and, at a public footpath sign to Daglingworth, turn left over a stile **C**, walk along the left-hand edge of a small tree nursery, cross a tarmac drive and turn right through a waymarked gate. Technically, the way continues beside the little Duntisbourne stream but this is physically difficult because of overgrown scrub. Instead, walk along a track and, at the corner of the scrub, turn right down to the stream and turn left to continue beside it along the right-hand edge of a field to a stile.

Climb the stile, walk along the right-hand field edge, following it as it bears right, and turn left through a metal gate. Head diagonally across the next field, making for a waymarked post on the far side, and bear right to keep along the left-hand field edge to a gate. Go through, continue across the next field towards farm buildings, climb a stile in the far right corner and bear left along a track between the farm

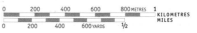

*The idyllic-looking hamlet of Duntisbourne Rouse*

buildings to a lane at Lower End **D**.

*Turn left along a track here, at a public bridleway sign, for the shorter walk.*

For the full walk, keep ahead and, where the lane turns right, go through a gate, walk along the right-hand field edge and go through another gate onto a track. Keep ahead, passing to the left of Daglingworth's medieval church, and bear right down into the village. At a crossroads turn left, follow the lane around a left-hand bend and take the first turning on the right, signposted 'The Duntisbournes and Youth Hostel'. Where the lane curves left, turn right **E** along a narrow lane that heads uphill and peters out into a rough track.

At this point, bear left onto a path, at a public bridleway sign to Duntisbourne Rouse, which continues up, passing behind cottages, to a gate. Go through, walk along the left-hand edge of two fields, by woodland on the left, and after going through a gate in the corner of the second field, there is a lovely view ahead over the valley to the idyllic village of Duntisbourne Rouse. Head downhill towards the village, go through a gate, turn left along a track and cross a footbridge over the stream by a ford. At a public footpath sign, turn right up steps, go through a gate, walk along an enclosed path and go through another gate into the church-yard **F**. The largely Norman church has a low saddleback tower at the west end, and the interior, delightfully simple and unspoilt, retains some medieval wall-paintings. So steep is the slope on which the church is built that there is a crypt at the east end.

From here, retrace your steps to Daglingworth and on past the church to where the route emerges onto a lane at Lower End. Just after joining the lane, turn right **D** at a public bridleway sign, along a broad track, here rejoining the shorter walk. Follow this gently undulating track across fields for the next 1¼ miles (2km) to the edge of Cirencester Park, a huge expanse of parkland that extends to the town centre of Cirencester. Do not enter the park but turn sharp left, at a public bridleway sign, onto another track **G**.

After ¾ mile (1.2km) you reach a crossing of tracks where you turn right **H** along a track that keeps along the right-hand edge of a field, by a hedge on the right, passing an isolated oak tree in the field. Follow the field edge as it curves left, turn right through a gate and continue along an enclosed path, which later becomes a tarmac track. Keep along it into Stratton and, at a public footpath sign, turn right along a track **B**. Here you rejoin the outward route and retrace your steps to the starting point. ●

# Banbury, Oxford Canal and Broughton

*Banbury, Oxford Canal and Broughton*

| | |
|---|---|
| **Start** | Banbury, the Cross |
| **Distance** | 10 miles (16km) |
| **Approximate time** | 4½ hours |
| **Parking** | Banbury |
| **Refreshments** | Pubs and cafés at Banbury, pubs at Bodicote, pub at Broughton |
| **Ordnance Survey maps** | Landranger 151 (Stratford-upon-Avon), Explorer 191 (Banbury, Bicester & Chipping Norton) |

*From the busy town centre of Banbury, the towpath of the Oxford Canal provides a quick and easy 'green corridor' into quiet countryside. The route continues along an ancient trackway – the Salt Way – and across fields to Broughton. After a brief incursion into Broughton Park, mainly for the classic view of the adjacent church and castle, the Salt Way is used again on the return leg before heading back to Banbury Cross.*

Despite recent expansion and modernisation, the narrow streets and alleys and the many fine old buildings – dating from the 15th to the 19th century – in the centre of Banbury are evidence of its past as a flourishing market town and important route centre. The walk starts at Banbury Cross, of nursery rhyme fame, which is a 19th-century replacement. Nearby is the large and imposing Georgian church, built in 1790.

🖉 Begin by turning down High Street (signposted Town Centre), at a fork continue along the left-hand street, passing to the right of the town hall, and keep ahead along Bridge Street. Cross the canal bridge but, before reaching the railway bridge, turn left onto a tarmac path **A** that bends left across a grassy area and at a fork take the left-hand path to the canal.

Turn left onto the towpath of the Oxford Canal, opened in 1790 to link Oxford with Coventry and the industrial Midlands. From the start it was a great commercial success but declined after the coming of the railways. Keep by the canal for the next 1½ miles (2.4km) as far as a brick-built bridge. The noise and bustle of the town is soon left behind as the canal proceeds through tranquil and pleasant countryside. At the bridge, go up steps and over a stile to the left of it and turn right to cross it **B**. This part of the route is waymarked 'Banbury Fringe Circular Walk'. Follow a track gently uphill, keep ahead to emerge onto a road at Bodicote and take the road ahead (Broad Gap) to a T-junction. The village centre, with its old church – mostly rebuilt in 1844 – and thatched cottages, is to the left but the route continues to the right.

| 0 | 200 | 400 | 600 | 800 METRES | 1 |
| 0 | 200 | 400 | 600 YARDS | ½ | KILOMETRES MILES |

Just before reaching a traffic island, turn left along a tree-lined track **C**. This is the Salt Way, part of an ancient route that ran from Droitwich, where the salt was produced, to the River Thames and on to London. Initially the track keeps along the edge of houses on the outskirts of Banbury and continues to a road **D**. Cross over, walk along the hedge- and tree-lined path opposite,

passing below Crouch Hill – the highest point in the vicinity – seen through the trees on the right. At a footpath post on the right, turn left **E** through a hedge gap, cross a plank footbridge over a ditch and bear slightly right across a field towards a farm.

Climb a stile in the field corner, keep ahead across the next field, passing to the left of the farm, and continue along the right-hand field edge. In the corner, turn right through a gate and walk along a hedge-lined path, curving left

through a hedge gap and then bearing right to keep along the left-hand edge of the next field. Go through a gate, turn left along the left-hand field edge and go through another gate onto a lane **F**. Turn right into Broughton, descending gently to a crossroads by the Saye and Sele Arms **G**.

The route continues to the right but turn left for a brief detour to see the church and castle and walk through part of Broughton Park. Turn right along a paved path to the church,

crossing Sor Brook and going through a gate into the churchyard. Broughton church was built in the early 14th century by Sir John de Broughton, who also built the nearby castle. It contains many fine tombs and monuments to the owners of the castle, the Broughton and later the Fiennes families. Keep along the path to the left of the church and go through a gate to enter Broughton Park. As you continue along a tarmac drive, there is to the left a splendid view of the moated castle in its fine parkland setting. Sir John de Broughton's original manor house was enlarged into a castle in the 15th century and subsequently converted into a more domestic and comfortable residence.

Where the drive bends right, keep ahead uphill across grassland and, after about 200 yds (183m), turn right – there is no visible path – and head down to climb a stone stile in the corner to the left of a lodge. Turn right along a lane to return to the crossroads by the pub Ⓖ and turn left along a road – be careful as there are no verges in places. About 200 yds (183m) after the road curves right, turn sharp right onto a hedge- and tree-lined track Ⓗ to rejoin the Salt Way.

The track narrows to a path, bends left and continues gently uphill, rejoining the outward route and continuing to a road Ⓓ. Turn left and follow it into the centre of Banbury, turning left at a T-junction to return to Banbury Cross.

*Banbury Cross*

# Tetbury and Westonbirt

| | |
|---|---|
| **Start** | Tetbury |
| **Distance** | 9½ miles (15.3km) |
| **Approximate time** | 4½ hours |
| **Parking** | Tetbury |
| **Refreshments** | Pubs and cafés at Tetbury |
| **Ordnance Survey maps** | Landrangers 162 (Gloucester & Forest of Dean) and 163 (Cheltenham & Cirencester), Explorer 168 (Stroud, Tetbury & Malmesbury) |

*Although a lengthy walk, it is relatively undemanding as it is across the almost flat terrain bordering the southern Cotswolds that lies to the south and west of Tetbury. The route passes by the imposing Westonbirt House – now a school – and at the approximate halfway point, it takes you across part of Westonbirt Arboretum. It is well worth paying the entrance fee for a fuller look at this vast and superb collection of trees. For much of the way, the slender spire of Tetbury church is in sight.*

Even by Cotswold standards, Tetbury is an outstandingly attractive town with a wealth of 17th- and 18th-century houses, built at the time when it was the centre for the local wool trade. The church is unusual in that, although dating from the late 18th century, it is built in the Gothic rather than the contemporary Georgian style. Its tall, slender spire is a landmark for miles around and it has a light and spacious interior. The walk starts in the market square by the 17th-century Market House.

📷 Facing the Market House and with your back to the Snooty Fox Hotel, turn first left and then right along Silver Street. The road curves left downhill and, after crossing the bridge over the infant River Avon, turn right **Ⓐ** along a tarmac track, at a public footpath sign. In front of a gate, turn right through a metal gate, keep ahead over a stile to

a T-junction and turn left to climb another stile.

Head uphill to enter a field, turn left and walk along the left-hand edge of the next three fields, climbing a succession of stiles. The route then continues along the right-hand edge of a field and, in the corner, turn right through a gate and walk across a narrow field to another gate. After going through that one, keep ahead across a field, pass through a gap and continue along the left-hand edge of the next field to a gate. Go through, keep ahead, passing between redundant gateposts, and in the next field, look out for where you turn left to cross a footbridge over the stream that you have been following for some time. Head uphill along the right-hand field edge, go through a gate, continue along the right-hand edge of the next field and, at a public footpath sign, turn right to follow a track along the right-hand field edge and through a gate onto a lane **B**.

Turn right and, at a public bridleway sign, turn left onto a track and follow this delightful tree-lined track (Wormwell Lane) to a lane. Take the lane opposite, signposted to Easton Grey, and at a public footpath sign turn right onto a track **C** and immediately climb a stile. Keep by the left-hand field edge, veering slightly right to go through a gate, and continue across the next two fields. Climb a stile in the corner of the second field, bear left through a gate and walk along a track, to the right of farm buildings. The track curves right, left and right again and at a yellow waymark, turn left. Go through

a gate and walk along the left-hand field edge.

Go through a gate, follow the track around left- and right-hand bends and continue, by a fence on the left, to go through another gate. Bear slightly right across a field, skirting the left-hand corner of woodland, and continue across to climb a stile on the far side onto a lane **D**. Climb the stone stile opposite, walk across a field to a way-marked gate, go through and keep in the same direction across the next two fields, climbing a stile. After going through a kissing-gate on the far side of the second field, continue across park-

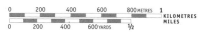

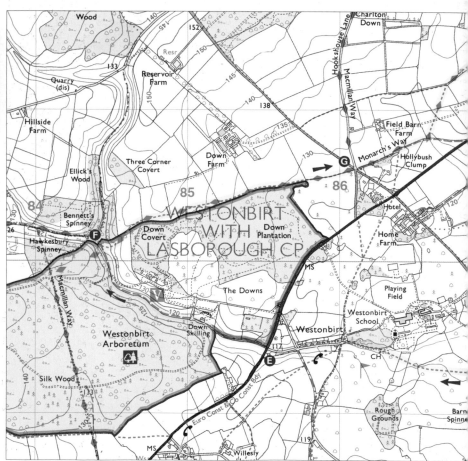

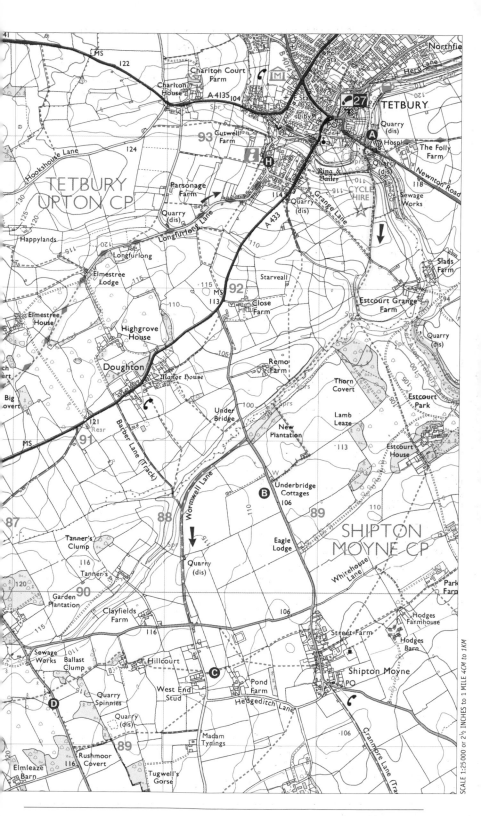

*The Market House at Tetbury*

right and head uphill to a gate in the field corner. After going through it, walk along the right-hand edge of a series of fields and through a succession of gates – by the left-hand edge of the arboretum all the while – eventually climbing a stile at the corner of the woodland. Keep ahead, by a wall on the left, and climb a stile onto a lane **G**.

land, aiming for a waymarked gate on the far side. Over to the right is an impressive view of the grand, 19th-century mansion of Westonbirt House, now a school.

Go through the gate, bear slightly right across the next field, climb a stile and bear right across the corner of a golf course to a tarmac track. Bear left along it to emerge onto a lane and keep ahead through Westonbirt village. At a crossroads, keep ahead to the A433 **E** cross over and take the enclosed, tree-lined path opposite through Westonbirt Arboretum. This magnificent collection of trees and shrubs of all kinds – over 18,000 – was started in 1829 and is being added to all the time. It looks spectacular and is worth a lengthy visit at any season of the year. There is a visitor centre, plant centre, gift shop and café, and an admission charge is payable at the entrance.

The path emerges onto a tarmac track. Keep ahead to a T-junction of tracks, go through a gate with a No Parking sign on it and continue along the right edge of Silk Wood. Cross a track, continue along the edge of the wood to a waymarked post **F**, turn

Go through the gate opposite, at a public bridleway sign, and walk along a hedge-lined track, going through two more gates. Continue along a left-hand field edge and look out for where you turn left over a stile. Head gently uphill across a field, climb a stone stile and continue in the same direction across the next field to climb another stone stile in the corner. Bear right along a grassy track – between a fence on the left and a hedge on the right – pass through a wall gap and continue along the right-hand field edge to a stone stile. Climb it, keep ahead across two fields, climbing a stile and crossing the drive to Elmestree House – seen on the left – to a gate in the corner.

After going through two gates in quick succession, walk across a field in the direction of a house, go through a gate on the far side, continue across the next field to join a track in the far corner and go through a gate. Keep ahead, passing to the right of a lodge, go through another gate and continue along a narrow, hedge- and tree-lined lane into Tetbury. At a T-junction, turn right **H** to the main road and turn left, passing the church, to return to the Market Place. ●

# Dursley, Uley and Owlpen

| | |
|---|---|
| **Start** | Dursley |
| **Distance** | 8½ miles (13.7km) |
| **Approximate time** | 4½ hours |
| **Parking** | Dursley |
| **Refreshments** | Pubs and cafés at Dursley, pub at Uley, pub at Woodmancote |
| **Ordnance Survey maps** | Landranger 162 (Gloucester & Forest of Dean), Explorer 167 (Thornbury, Dursley & Yate) |

*There are plenty of 'ups and downs' – some of them steep – on this lengthy, varied and quite energetic walk, especially on the first part as you follow the Cotswold Way along the escarpment from Dursley, over Peaked Down and Cam Long Down. After descending into Uley, the route follows a quiet lane into the secluded hamlet of Owlpen. The rest of the walk is beside the little River Ewelme and along the edge of woodland, with a final climb through Hermitage Wood to return to the start. A thoroughly enjoyable and absorbing walk with superb views all the way.*

Dursley lies below the well-wooded Cotswold escarpment on the edge of the Vale of Berkeley. The town is centred on the dignified 18th-century Market House and imposing medieval church. The tower of the latter had to be rebuilt in the early 18th century after the collapse of its predecessor.

The walk starts by the Market House. Turn down Long Street and, where the road bends left, bear right to continue along a track to a kissing-gate. Go through, climb steps through woodland, go through another kissing-gate at the top and walk across a field to climb a stile. Turn left along the left-hand edge of the next two fields, climbing a stile, turn left over another stile and continue along the right-hand field edge.

Climb a stile onto a lane, turn right and, on reaching a lane on the right signposted to Uley, bear right **Ⓐ** to climb a stile at a Cotswold Way sign. Walk across a field to climb another one, continue across the next field and go through a metal gate in front of a farm. Turn right along a lane and, where it curves left, turn right through a gate and head uphill through trees. Take the left-hand upper path at a fork, cross a tarmac drive and continue steeply uphill over Peaked Down.

Descend towards trees, bearing slightly right to enter the woodland at a Cotswold Way post. Head uphill again to emerge onto open grassland and continue over the top of Cam Long Down (722ft/220m), a magnificent ridge walk with extensive views on both sides and ahead. At the end of the ridge, descend steeply through woodland, following a winding, stepped path down

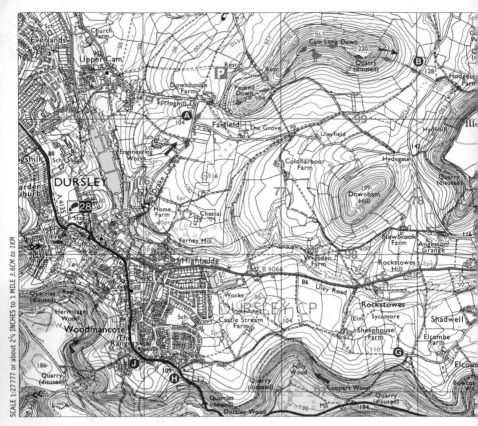

to a stile. After climbing it, descend more steps to emerge from the trees, continue steeply downhill between bracken and walk across a field to climb a stile at a hedge corner. Keep along the left-hand edge of the next field, climb a stile and continue along a narrow lane **B**.

Where the lane turns right, turn left along a track, at a public bridleway sign to Uley Bury and Frocester Hill, which bears right and heads uphill, passing between farms. It then continues steeply uphill through trees to pass beside a gate onto a road. Just before the road, turn right **C** beside a metal gate, at a public bridleway sign, along a broad, tree-lined track and, on emerging from the trees, turn left onto a path that keeps by the earthworks of Uley Bury, the site of a prehistoric settlement now covered by crops.

Look out for a fork, at a public bridleway sign, where you take the left-hand, lower path, which descends quite steeply to enter woodland. Continue down through this delightful woodland, passing by a redundant stile, take the left-hand path at another fork, and the path winds down to a gate. Go through and continue downhill along the top edge of a sloping field, bearing right away from the field edge to a kissing-gate. Go through, keep ahead along an enclosed path and turn left alongside the churchyard wall at Uley to a road. The church is a fine Victorian building but the 18th-century houses in this now quiet village are a reflection of its heyday as a busy centre of cloth production.

Turn left and, by the Old Crown pub, bear right along Fiery Lane **D**, sign-posted to Owlpen, and follow it for ½ mile (800m) into the secluded hamlet. Here the lane curves right to pass by the

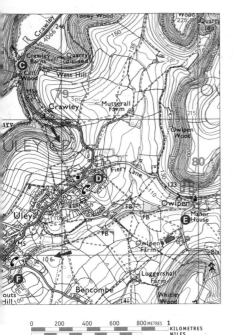

```
0    200  400  600  800 METRES  1
0    200  400  600 YARDS  ½      ½
```
KILOMETRES
MILES

the right-hand field edge, by a fence or the right, follow the edge to the left climb a stile in the corner.

Immediately climb another one, ahead by the right-hand field edge, right over a stile, bear left across the corner of the next field and climb another stile. Head gently uphill along the right-hand edge of the next field and climb a stile onto a track. Turn right, bear left off the track and, at a sign 'Public Path', turn left along an enclosed path **G**. The next part of the walk may be overgrown but conditions improve as the path climbs steadily between steep, wooded embankments. At the top, take the right-hand track at a fork and continue through the attractive Coopers Wood, keeping close to its right-hand edge. Where the track turns left, keep ahead along a sunken path by the right, inside edge of the wood, cross a track and continue along a hedge-lined path which eventually heads up to a road **H**.

Turn right downhill and, just after passing the New Inn, turn left along Nunnery Lane **J**. At a fork, take the right-hand, uphill lane and, where it ends, keep ahead along a steeply ascending and enclosed path by the right, inside edge of woodland. At a footpath post, turn right, in the direction of the public bridleway, along a winding track that continues by the right, inside edge of Hermitage Wood to a T-junction. Turn right downhill along a sunken path to emerge from the wood and continue downhill along a lane.

At a public footpath sign just before reaching a T-junction, turn left along an enclosed tarmac path that turns right and continues to a road. Keep ahead for about 100 yds (91m) along Upper Poole Road and, at a crossroads, turn right – No Through Road sign here – along a road to a T-junction. Turn left to return to the starting point. ●

Tudor manor-house and below the 19th-century church, a delightful combination lying at the foot of a wooded hillside and above the little River Ewelme. At a public footpath sign, turn right over a stile **E** – the stile ahead not the one on the right – and continue across a series of meadows and over a succession of stiles, by the River Ewelme on the right. In the tapering corner of the last meadow, cross a footbridge over a brook, head uphill and continue across more fields and through a succession of kissing-gates, finally climbing a stile in the last field corner onto an enclosed path.

Keep along the path, over a track and on through trees, to a road, turn right and take the first lane on the left, signposted to Shadwell and Elcombe **F**. The lane bends right and, where it curves left, bear right, at a public footpath sign, along a tree-lined track. Keep to the left of a house, bear right to climb a stile and walk diagonally across a field to the far right corner. Do not climb the stile there but turn left along

# Further Information

 ## The National Trust

Anyone who likes visiting places of natural beauty and/or historic interest has cause to be grateful to the National Trust. Without it, many such places would probably have vanished by now.

It was in response to the pressures on the countryside posed by the relentless march of Victorian industrialisation that the trust was set up in 1895. Its founders, inspired by the common goals of protecting and conserving Britain's national heritage and widening public access to it, were Sir Robert Hunter, Octavia Hill and Canon Rawnsley: respectively a solicitor, a social reformer and a clergyman. The latter was particularly influential. As a canon of Carlisle Cathedral and vicar of Crosthwaite (near Keswick), he was concerned about threats to the Lake District and had already been active in protecting footpaths and promoting public access to open countryside. After the flooding of Thirlmere in 1879 to create a large reservoir, he became increasingly convinced that the only effective way to guarantee protection was outright ownership of land.

The purpose of the National Trust is to preserve areas of natural beauty and sites of historic interest by acquisition, holding them in trust for the nation and making them available for public access and enjoyment. Some of its properties have been acquired through purchase, but many of the Trust's properties have been donated. Nowadays it is not only one of the biggest landowners in the country, but also one of the most active conservation charities, protecting 581,113 acres (253,176 ha) of land, including 555 miles (892km) of coastline, and over 300 historic properties in England, Wales and Northern Ireland. (There is a separate National Trust for Scotland, which was set up in 1931.)

Furthermore, once a piece of land has come under National Trust ownership, it is difficult for its status to be altered. As a result of parliamentary legislation in 1907, the Trust was given the right to declare its property inalienable, so ensuring that in any subsequent dispute it can appeal directly to parliament.

As it works towards its dual aims of conserving areas of attractive countryside and encouraging greater public access (not easy to reconcile in this age of mass tourism), the Trust provides an excellent service for walkers by creating new concessionary paths and waymarked trails, maintaining stiles and foot bridges and combating the ever-increasing problem of footpath erosion.

For details of membership, contact the National Trust at the address on page 94.

 ## The Ramblers' Association

No organisation works more actively to protect and extend the rights and interests of walkers in the countryside than the Ramblers' Association. Its aims are clear: to foster a greater knowledge, love and care of the countryside; to assist in the protection and enhancement of public rights of way and areas of natural beauty; to work for greater public access to the countryside; and to encourage more people to take up rambling as a healthy, recreational leisure activity.

It was founded in 1935 when, following the setting up of a National Council of Ramblers' Federations in 1931, a number of federations earlier formed in London, Manchester, the Midlands and elsewhere came together to create a more effective pressure group, to deal with such problems as the disappearance and obstruction of footpaths, the prevention of access to open mountain and moorland and increasing hostility from landowners. This was the era of the mass trespasses, when there were sometimes violent confrontations between ramblers and gamekeepers, especially on the moorlands of the Peak District.

Since then the Ramblers' Association has played an influential role in preserving and developing the national footpath network, supporting the creation of national parks and encouraging the designation and waymarking of long-distance routes.

Our freedom to walk in the countryside is precarious and requires constant vigilance. As well as the perennial problems of footpaths being illegally obstructed, disappearing through lack of use or extinguished by housing or road construction, new dangers can spring up at any time.

It is to meet such problems and dangers that the Ramblers' Association exists and represents the interests of all walkers. The address to write to for information on the Ramblers' Association and how to become a member is given on page 94.

*Near Charlbury*

### Walkers and the Law

The average walker in a national park or other popular walking area, armed with the appropriate Ordnance Survey map, reinforced perhaps by a guidebook giving detailed walking instructions, is unlikely to run into legal difficulties, but it is useful to know something about the law relating to public rights of way. The right to walk over certain parts of the countryside has developed over a long period, and how such rights came into being is a complex subject, too lengthy to be discussed here. The following comments are intended simply as a helpful guide, backed up by the Countryside Access Charter, a concise summary of walkers' rights and obligations drawn up by the Countryside Agency (see page 92).

Basically there are two main kinds of public rights of way: footpaths (for walkers only) and bridleways (for walkers,

riders on horseback and pedal cyclists). Footpaths and bridleways are shown by broken green lines on Ordnance Survey Explorer maps and broken red lines on Landranger maps. There is also a third category, called byways: chiefly broad tracks (green lanes) or farm roads, which walkers, riders and cyclists have to share, usually only occasionally, with motor vehicles. Many of these public paths have been in existence for hundreds of years and some even originated as prehistoric trackways and have been in constant use for well over 2,000 years. Ways known as RUPPs (roads used as public paths) still appear on some maps. The legal definition of such byways is ambiguous and they are gradually being reclassified as footpaths, bridleways or byways.

The term 'right of way' means exactly what it says. It gives right of passage over what, in the vast majority of cases, is private land, and you are required to keep to the line of the path and not stray on to the land on either side. If you inadvertently wander off the right of way – either because of faulty map-reading or because the route is not clearly indicated on the ground – you are technically trespassing and the wisest course is to ask the nearest available person (farmer or fellow walker) to direct you back to the correct route. There are stories about unpleasant confrontations between walkers and farmers at times, but in general most farmers are co-operative when responding to a

**Countryside Access Charter**

*Your rights of way are:*

- public footpaths – on foot only. Sometimes waymarked in yellow
- bridleways – on foot, horseback and pedal cycle. Sometimes waymarked in blue
- byways (usually old roads), most 'roads used as public paths' and, of course, public roads – all traffic has the right of way

Use maps, signs and waymarks to check rights of way. Ordnance Survey Explorer and Landranger maps show most public rights of way

*On rights of way you can:*

- take a pram, pushchair or wheelchair if practicable
- take a dog (on a lead or under close control)
- take a short route round an illegal obstruction or remove it sufficiently to get past

*You have a right to go for recreation to:*

- public parks and open spaces – on foot
- most commons near older towns and cities – on foot and sometimes on horseback
- private land where the owner has a formal agreement with the local authority

*In addition you can use the following by local or established custom or consent, but ask for advice if you are unsure:*

- many areas of open country, such as moorland, fell and coastal areas, especially those in the care of the National Trust, and some commons
- some woods and forests, especially those owned by the Forestry Commission
- country parks and picnic sites
- most beaches
- canal towpaths
- some private paths and tracks Consent sometimes extends to horse-riding and cycling

*For your information:*

- county councils and London boroughs maintain and record rights of way, and register commons
- obstructions, dangerous animals, harassment and misleading signs on rights of way are illegal and you should report them to the county council
- paths across fields can be ploughed, but must normally be reinstated within two weeks
- landowners can require you to leave land to which you have no right of access
- motor vehicles are normally permitted only on roads, byways and some 'roads used as public paths'

genuine and polite request for assistance in route-finding.

Obstructions can sometimes be a problem and probably the most common of these is where a path across a field has been ploughed up. It is legal for a farmer to plough up a path provided that he restores it within two weeks, barring exceptionally bad weather. This does not always happen and here the walker is presented with a dilemma: to follow the line of the path, even if this inevitably means treading on crops, or to walk around the edge of the field. The latter course of action often seems the best but this means that you would be trespassing and not keeping to the exact line of the path. In the case of other obstructions

which may block a path (illegal fences and locked gates etc), common sense has to be used in order to negotiate them by the easiest method – detour or removal. You should only ever remove as much as is necessary to get through, and if you can easily go round the obstruction without causing any damage, then you should do so. If you have any problems negotiating rights of way, you should report the matter to the rights of way department of the relevant council, which will take action with the landowner concerned.

Apart from rights of way enshrined by law, there are a number of other paths available to walkers. Permissive or concessionary paths have been created where a landowner has given permission for the public to use a particular route across his land. The main problem with these is that, as they have been granted as a concession, there is no legal right to use them and therefore they can be extinguished at any time. In practice, many of these concessionary routes have been established on land owned either by large public bodies such as the Forestry Commission, or by a private one, such as the National Trust, and as these mainly encourage walkers to use their paths, they are unlikely to be closed unless a change of ownership occurs.

Walkers also have free access to country parks (except where requested to keep away from certain areas for ecological reasons, e.g wildlife protection, woodland regeneration, etc), canal towpaths and most beaches. By custom, though not by right, you are generally free to walk across the open and uncultivated higher land of mountain, moorland and fell, but this varies from area to area and from one season to another – grouse moors, for example, will be out of bounds during the breeding and shooting seasons and some open areas are used as Ministry of Defence firing ranges, for which reason access will be restricted. In some areas the situation has been clarified as a result of

'access agreements' between the landowners and either the county council or the national park authority, which clearly define when and where you can walk over such open country.

 ## Walking Safety

Although the reasonably gentle countryside that is the subject of this book offers no real dangers to walkers at any time of the year, it is still advisable to take sensible precautions and follow certain well-tried guidelines.

Always take with you both warm and waterproof clothing and sufficient food and drink. Wear suitable footwear, such as strong walking boots or shoes that give a good grip over stony ground, on slippery slopes and in muddy conditions. Try to obtain a local weather forecast and bear it in mind before you start. Do not be afraid to abandon your proposed route and return to your starting point in the event of a sudden and unexpected deterioration in the weather.

All the walks described in this book will be safe to do, given due care and respect, even during the winter. Indeed, a crisp, fine winter day often provides perfect walking conditions, with firm

*Near Painswick*

ground underfoot and a clarity unique to this time of the year.

The most difficult hazard likely to be encountered is mud, especially when walking along woodland and field paths, farm tracks and bridleways – the latter in particular can often get churned up by cyclists and horses. In summer, an additional difficulty may be narrow and overgrown paths, particularly along the edges of cultivated fields. Neither should constitute a major problem provided that the appropriate footwear is worn.

## The Cotswold Voluntary Warden Service

The Cotswold Voluntary Warden Service was formed in 1968 in order to assist in the preservation and promotion of the Cotswolds Area of Outstanding Natural Beauty.

The principal objectives of the Warden Service are: to provide facilities which improve public access and enjoyment of the countryside; to promote the qualities of the countryside, thereby enhancing the public's appreciation of them; and to protect the countryside from excessive, potentially damaging use.

The service is administered by Cotswold County Council. Further information can be obtained from: Cotswold Conservation Board, The old Police Station, Cotswold Heritage Centre, Northleach, Gloucestershire GL54 3JH.
Tel. 01451 862000

## Useful Organisations

**Campaign to Protect Rural England**
128 Southwark Street,
London SE1 0SW
Tel. 020 7981 2800
www.cpre.org.uk

**Countryside Agency**
John Dower House, Crescent Place,
Cheltenham, Gloucestershire GL50 3RA
Tel. 01242 521381
www.countryside.gov.uk

**Forestry Commission**
Silvan House, 231 Corstorphine Road,
Edinburgh EH12 7AT
Tel. 0131 334 0303
www.forestry.gov.uk

**Long Distance Walkers' Association**
Bank House, High Street, Wrotham,
Sevenoaks, Kent TN15 7AE
Tel. 01732 883705

**National Trust**
*Membership and general enquiries:*
PO Box 39, Warrington, WA5 7WD
Tel. 0870 458 4000
www.thenationaltrust.org.uk

**Ordnance Survey**
Romsey Road, Maybush,
Southampton SO16 4GU
Tel. 08456 05 05 05 (Lo-call)

**Ramblers' Association**
2nd Floor, Camelford House, 87-90 Albert Embankment, London SE1 7TW
Tel. 020 7339 8500
www.ramblers.org.uk

**Heart of England Tourist Board**
Woodside, Larkhill Road,
Worcester WR5 2EZ
Tel. 01905 761100
www.visitheartofengland.com
*Local tourist information offices* (*not open all year):
Abingdon: 01235 522711
Banbury: 01295 259855
Bath: 01225 477101
*Broadway: 01386 852937
Burford: 01993 823558
Cheltenham: 01242 522878
Chippenham: 01249 706333
Chipping Campden: 01386 840101
Chipping Norton: 01608 644379
Cirencester: 01285 654180
Evesham: 01386 446944
Gloucester: 01452 421188
Moreton-in-the-Marsh: 01608 650881
*Northleach: 01451 860715
Painswick: 01452 832532
Stow-on-the-Wold: 01451 831082
Stroud: 01453 760960

Tetbury: 01666 503552
Tewkesbury: 01684 295027
*Winchcombe: 01242 602925
Witney: 01993 775802
Woodstock: 01993 813276

**Youth Hostels Association**
Trevelyan House, Dimple Road,
Matlock, Derbyshire, DE4 3YH
Tel. 01629 592600
www.yha.org.uk

### Ordnance Survey maps of the Cotswolds

The area of *More Cotswold Walks* is
covered by Ordnance Survey 1:50 000
($1^1/_4$ inches to 1 mile or 2cm to 1km) scale
Landranger map sheets 150, 151, 162,
163, 164, 172, 173. These all-purpose
maps are packed with information to help
you explore the area. Viewpoints, picnic
sites, places of interest, caravan and
camping sites are shown, as well as public
rights of way information such as
footpaths and bridleways.

To examine the Cotswolds in more
detail and especially if you are planning
walks, Ordnance Survey Explorer maps at
1:25 000 ($2^1/_2$ inches to 1 mile or 4cm to

1km) scale are ideal:

155 Bristol & Bath
156 Chippenham & Bradford-on-Avon
157 Marlborough & Savernake Forest
158 Newbury & Hungerford
167 Thornbury, Dursley & Yate
168 Stroud, Tetbury & Malmesbury
169 Cirencester & Swindon
170 Abingdon, Wantage & Vale of White
    Horse
179 Gloucester, Cheltenham & Stroud
180 Oxford
191 Banbury, Bicester & Chipping Norton

Also at 1:25 000 scale ($2^1/_2$ inches to 1 mile
or 4cm to 1km) Explorer OL maps are
invaluable for walkers:

OL14 Wye Valley & Forest of Dean
OL45 The Cotswolds

To get to the Cotswolds use the Ordnance
Survey OS Travel-Map Route Great Britain
at 1:625 000 (1 inch to 10 miles or 4cm to
25 km) scale.

For touring, the OS Travel-Map Tour 8
(The Cotswolds & Gloucestershire) at a
scale of 1:100 000 (1cm to 1km or 1 inch
to $1^1/_2$ miles) is ideal.

Ordnance Survey maps and guides
are available from most booksellers,
stationers and newsagents.

*Chastleton House*

# www.totalwalking.co.uk

**www.totalwalking.co.uk**
is the official website of the Jarrold
Pathfinder and Short Walks guides. This
interactive website features a wealth of
information for walkers – from the latest
news on route diversions and advice from
professional walkers to product news, free
sample walks and promotional offers.

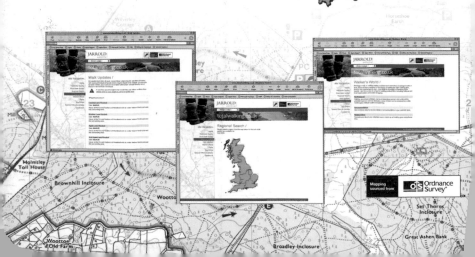